de fed:

L

G

G000231187

MILESTONES IN WORKING CLA

MILESTONES
IN
WORKING CLASS HISTORY

Norman Longmate

British Broadcasting Corporation

Published to accompany a series of 6 television programmes
first broadcast on BBC 1 at 11.05 pm on Thursday of each
week starting 6 November 1975
Produced: John Radcliffe

Published to accompany a series of programmes prepared in
consultation with the BBC Further Education Advisory
Council.

© Norman Longmate 1975
First published 1975

Published by the British Broadcasting Corporation
35 Marylebone High Street, London W1M 4AA

This book is set in 11pt Baskerville 169
Printed in England by Lowe & Brydone (Printers) Ltd,
Thetford, Norfolk

ISBN 0 563 10968 8

Contents

Acknowledgment is due to the following for permission to reproduce illustrations

BARNABY'S PICTURE LIBRARY Wensleydale knitters (Bernard Alfieri), page 12; BARRATT'S PHOTO PRESS John Maclean, page 107; THE BRONTË SOCIETY William Cartwright, page 59; CAMERA PRESS LTD women demonstrating (Blye/Paine), page 151, demonstration (G/M), page 152, dockers demonstrating (Les Wilson), page 153; CENTRAL OFFICE OF INFORMATION (CROWN COPYRIGHT) Congress House, page 155; CENTRAL PRESS PHOTOS LTD civil servants demonstrating, page 151, Harold Wilson, page 154; CONTROLLER, H.M.S.O. (CROWN COPYRIGHT) record of execution (H.O.42/132), page 61; CROWN COPYRIGHT *In Place of Strife*, page 153; MARY EVANS PICTURE LIBRARY cotton mill, page 19, Luddites plotting, page 47, William Horsfall's murder, page 57, match girls' procession, page 70; FOX PHOTOS unloading milk, page 139, society ladies, page 140, strike scene, page 141; GLASGOW HERALD AND EVENING TIMES W. M. Gallacher, page 107, Lloyd George, page 123, Red flag in George Square, page 130, tanks, page 131, trial, page 132; JOHN GORMAN banner, page 72; HODDER AND STOUGHTON cartoon, page 73 (from *A Match to Fire the Thames* by Ann Stafford; IMPERIAL WAR MUSEUM, LONDON appeal board, page 149; KEEPER OF THE RECORDS OF SCOTLAND Renfrew Yards (Lobnitz Collection), page 103, train ferry under construction (Fairfield Collection), page 105, hoisting gun barrel (Clydebank Collection), page 112 (all from *Clyde Shipbuilding* introd. John R. Hume and Michael S. Moss, pub. B. T. Batsford Ltd.), ship being launched (Fairfield Collection), page 104, women munitions workers (John Brown Collection), page 127 (by courtesy of Department of Economic History, University of Glasgow); KEYSTONE PRESS AGENCY Edward Heath, page 154, Trades Union Congress, page 155; KIRKLESS METROPOLITAN COUNCIL Enoch's hammer, page 44, cropper's bench, cropping shears, page 48, John Wood's cropping shop, page 49, Shear's Inn, page 50, Dumb Steeple, page 53, Huddersfield Cloth Hall, page 56, Sir Joseph Radcliffe, page 59; LABOUR PARTY PHOTOGRAPH LIBRARY David Kirkwood, front and back covers and page 107, posters, page 134; MANCHESTER PUBLIC LIBRARIES Market Street, Manchester, page 15, Samuel Bamford, page 17, mill operatives, front and back covers and page 35; THE MANSELL COLLECTION Hat Finishers pictorial heading, cartoon, page 8, William Cobbett, page 17, Sheffield, page 18, Bethnal Green slums, page 20, Sheffield, page 21, London slum, page 22, stocking factory, page 23, children for hire, page 26, cutlery manufacture, page 31, factory hands, page 33, coal mine, page 34, Rawfolds Mill, page 52, Luddite riot, front and back covers and page 54, London slum interior, page 67, dockers waiting for work, page 69, gas workers' meeting, page 71, Finance Committee meeting, page 80, dockers' wives and sweethearts, page 84, dockers, page 85, Docks at night by Doré, page 89, *For Services Rendered* and *Traitor* cartoons, page 110, cartoon, page 145; MITCHELL LIBRARY, GLASGOW Sir William Beardmore, front and back covers and page 108, call to arms, page 109, cartoons from *Forward*, page 110, tool room, page 122; NATIONAL MARITIME MUSEUM, LONDON S.W. India Dock, page 63, landing meat at dock, page 65; NATIONAL PORTRAIT GALLERY, LONDON Earl Fitzwilliam, page 59; NORTH WESTERN MUSEUM OF SCIENCE AND INDUSTRY silk loom, page 14; NOTTINGHAMSHIRE COUNTY COUNCIL LOCAL STUDIES LIBRARY reward notice, page 41; PORT OF LONDON AUTHORITY distributing food tickets, page 8, dockers' children, page 85, Manning cartoon, page 96; PUBLIC RECORD OFFICE reward notice (H.O.40/1/1), page 45, Ned Ludd letter (H.O.42/122), page 60; RADIO TIMES HULTON PICTURE LIBRARY basketmakers, page 13, riding the stang, page 16, William Lovett, page 17, Francis Place, page 17, casting a cylinder, page 32, King Ludd caricature, page 38, rick burning, page 43, Lord Sidmouth, page 59, London docks, page 64, London slum exterior, page 66, John Burns addressing meeting, page 74, soup kitchen, page 83, Conciliation Committee, page 92, Thomas Mann, John Burns, Ben Tillett, William Thorne, page 94, return to work, page 98, demonstration of military force, page 131, outside pawnshop, man with sandwich board, page 135, leaders of first Labour Government, page 136, miners, page 137, strikers' meeting, page 142, soldiers unloading lorry, page 143, food convoy, page 144, Ernest Bevin, Stanley Baldwin, Winston Churchill, page 146, schoolmasters' protest, page 147; SCIENCE MUSEUM, LONDON Coalbrookdale by night, page 10; STRATHCLYDE REGIONAL ARCHIVES Glasgow street, page 100, miners' rows at Netherton, page 102; SYNDICATION INTERNATIONAL bus-loads of constables, page 143; TOPIX demonstrating outside Lloyds Bank, page 157; TRADES UNION CONGRESS manifesto, page 79, dock workers' emblem, page 82, Arthur Cook, page 138, Walter Citrine, page 146, T.U.C. training, page 157; TRANSPORT AND GENERAL WORKERS' UNION dock workers' procession, front and back covers and page 75; UNIVERSITY COURT, UNIVERSITY OF GLASGOW AND DEPARTMENT OF ECONOMIC HISTORY BUSINESS ARCHIVES (HERBERT HIGHTON COLLECTION) Clyde Workers' Committee rules, pages 118 and 119, manifesto, page 128; THE WEIR GROUP LTD Sir William Weir, page 114; ROBERT WOOD factory rules and regulations, page 24.

Acknowledgment is also due to the following:

GEORGE G. HARRAP & CO. LTD. for extracts from *My life of revolt* by David Kirkwood; HUTCHINSON PUBLISHING GROUP for extracts from *Behind the steam* by Betty Meyrick; LAWRENCE & WISHART LTD. for extracts from *Revolt on the Clyde* by William Gallacher. *The story of the docker's strike* by Sir Hubert Llewellyn Smith and Vaughan Nash was published by T. Fisher Unwin in 1889.

The captions for the following photographs are page 10, Coalbrookdale by night. Page 29, 'at the pub.' An early nineteenth century drawing. Page 34, Underground at Bradley mine near Bolston, Staffordshire. Page 35, Manchester cotton workers. Page 47, A Luddite leader, addresses potential recruits at an inn. Page 152, Industrial Relations Bill, 1971. Page 153, Demonstrating against the imprisonment of dock workers 1972.

Introduction

This book examines in some detail three episodes in British industrial history and endeavours to set them in their social and political context. It makes no claim to be a history of the working class during the period covered, nor, in the three periods examined, to deal with any groups of workers other than those directly involved in them. Since all these were town-dwellers, the book is concerned solely with urban life and industrial unions; the situation, and problems, of the agricultural labourer, though full of interest in their own right, are outside its scope.

Although the book is designed to accompany a series of programmes produced by the BBC Further Education Department and first shown on BBC Television in the Autumn of 1975, it is not directly derived from the programmes, though both programmes and book have inevitably to some extent drawn on the same source material and illustrations. I have incorporated a number of suggestions made by the producers of the series but the treatment of the subject-matter and the opinions expressed are my own.

I should like to record my appreciation of the assistance I have received from the staff of the BBC, particularly Mr John Radcliffe, producer of the associated television series, Miss Dianne Farris, who did much of the research for it, and Miss Doreen Jones, who collected illustrations for the book. I am also much in the debt of Miss Idina Le Geyt who did research specifically for the book.

June 1975   N.R.L.

WE ASSIST EACH OTHER IN TIME OF NEED.

A MEETING OF THE TRADES' UNIONS.

8

1 An end to these unions

It is very well known that the whole country is in a stir with what are called TRADES UNIONS. . . . The government newspapers have been recommending the Parliament to pass a law to put an end to these unions. Better call for a law to prevent those inconvenient things called *Spring tides*.

William Cobbett, *Political Register*, 7th December 1833

Few texts were more popular with nineteenth century preachers than St. Matthew, Chapter 26, Verse 11: 'For ye have the poor always with you'. These words seemed to justify both the manifest inequalities in society and an attitude of indifference towards them, though such a conclusion was misleading, for Christ had gone on to say, 'But me ye have not always'. The message was not that one could ignore one's duty to one's poorer neighbour but that there could exist even higher obligations. But this was conviently forgotten. The Bible was quoted as implying divine approval for the inevitable and perpetual existence of a large body of people suffering from want and hardship.

Who around 1810, the date of the first episode described in this book, *were* the poor? The answer no doubt depended upon one's own particular location in the social structure. Apart from those at the very bottom of the pyramid, for whom self respect and self-deception were luxuries they could not afford, most people probably regarded 'the poor' as those a little lower down the scale than themselves. Indisputably they included actual paupers, i.e. those who needed 'outdoor' parish relief, or admission to the workhouse to survive, and the 'poor' by this test totalled at any one time about a million in a population, excluding Ireland, of in 1811 just under 12,600,000. Extending the definition to include those for whom a single week's loss of earnings spelt disaster, the formula applied by later researchers, 'the poor' probably numbered at least five million. If one included those unable to cope unaided with a long spell of illness or loss of work due to a particularly hard Winter, the number must have included almost all those who worked with their hands, excluding only the most highly paid craftsmen.

In what were commonly called 'the middle ranks of society' the range of occupations, and the number of families, was comparatively small. The Industrial Revolution, beginning around 1760, and gathering strength from about 1780, when power-driven machinery began to come into widespread use in the cotton mills, had not yet progressed far enough to create that large middle-class army which was to be such a feature of Victorian England. Historians have referred in every century from the Middle Ages onwards to 'the rising middle class' but by 1810 it had not, by later standards, risen very far. There were some unmistakably middle-class groups, physicians, attorneys, clergy, schoolmasters—but industrial and commercial organisation was still on too small a scale to require many clerks and managers. Government departments were tiny and local authorities little larger, while new industries like the railways, which provided thousands of 'white collar jobs', as well as manual employment, were not yet launched. The first steam train was not to puff from Stockton to Darlington for another fifteen years.

Easiest of all to identify were the 'higher orders of society', whose power and status, as in feudal times, derived from the ownership of land. The 'country gentlemen' were less an important pressure group in the House of Commons—still, of course, unreformed— than the House itself. At least outside the towns, a magistrate was, almost by definition, a land-owner. And those who did not directly own or administer estates usually derived their income from them in some way. The conscientious land-owner may well have had a warmer relationship with his own labourers and their families, whose place in society was securely established, than with his bailiff or attorney or village schoolmaster who occupied the uneasy hinterland between the upper and lower classes; the expression 'working class' was rarely used, though it appears in Cobbett, along with some of the alternatives quoted, later, as early as 1817. To the upper classes the distinctions between different sections of the working class seemed too subtle to merit consideration. The highly-paid and literate printer—highly-paid indeed precisely because he *was* literate, unlike most of his fellow-working men— the independent-minded weaver owning his own loom, the mechanic tending a factory steam-engine, the skilled hedger and ditcher, in demand over several counties, the half-

starved farm labourer, not much in demand anywhere, and the 'hawker, huckster, pedlar, duffer', to take one census category, tramping from door to door pack on back, all seemed to their 'betters' a single vast mass, unenfranchised, unorganised, uneducated and—in the last resort—unimportant.

In 1814, one pioneer sociologist Patrick Colquhoun published in the *Wealth, Power and Resources of the British Empire* an estimate of the class breakdown of the inhabitants of Great Britain and of the amount received annually by each category. The results are clearly unreliable—he assumed, for example, a population of around 14 million, when England, Wales and Scotland, in fact contained 12,725,000, and, if Ireland were added, 18,923,000—but, if virtually a guess, it is at least a contemporary one.

Class	Estimated numbers	Estimated income
		£
The Aristocracy and their dependants, including servants	425,000	60,000,000
People employed in the public service or receiving state pensions	500,000	8,000,000
The Professions		17,000,000
Landowners, apart from the aristocracy, including farmers	3,000,000	74,000,000
Traders and other employers	750,000	37,000,000
Innkeepers and Publicans	437,000	9,000,000
The Working Classes, including artisans and labourers	9,000,000	82,000,000
Paupers, vagrants and criminals		10,000,000
Totals:	14,112,000	297,000,000

Clearly the population figures for all these groups, except the last, are misleading, since they include servants and their families, who, except perhaps for a few governesses, bailiffs and poor relations, properly belong to the bottom one, so that the true figure for the working class should be around ten million, i.e. rather over two thirds of the population. Even accepting Colquhoun's figures, however, the sharing out of the national income was palpably inequitable. The working class, forming two thirds of the population, received less than one third of the nation's wealth, and only half as much again as the aristocracy (defined as the 'nobility, gentry, royalty and upper clergy') though they outnumbered them by twenty to one. Similarly the farmers and other land-owners received nearly twenty-five per cent, almost as much as the working classes, even excluding domestic servants, though only one third of their number. Few of those who joined a trade union or a political club around the end of the Napoleonic wars can have been familiar with Colquhoun's figures, but, however dimly, many must have been aware that their share of the country's wealth was ill-related to their contribution to it, and that some drastic reorganisation of society seemed called for.

The working class had, however, no real awareness of its own identity; between operative and craftsman, labourer and artisan, was a gulf that only shared affliction or danger could bridge. It would have been in vain for the trumpet to have sounded summoning its members to a class war for most of those who heard it would not have known on which side they were expected to enrol.

Movement between the classes was still common. The most influential figure in the working-class movement of this generation was Francis Place, from an impeccably working-class background. In childhood—he had been born in 1771 so was aged forty in 1811—he had been apprenticed to a breeches-maker after his drunken father had offered him to anyone who would take him off his hands, but had risen to be a master tailor with an income of £3,000 a year. The staunchest champions of the working class rejected the very idea that they existed as a separate group, with interests of their own. In April 1817 William Cobbett, in the *Political Register,* fired a typical salvo against the country gentlemen, whom he accused of just such an attitude:

It has come into the heads of these people . . . a notion that it is proper to consider the labouring classes as *a distinct caste.* They are called nowadays, by these gents, 'The Peasantry'. This is a new term as applied to Englishmen. It is a French word, which, in its literal sense, means *Country Folk.* But in the sense in which it is used in France and Flanders and Germany, it means not only country people . . . but also a *distinct and degraded* class of persons, who have no pretensions whatever to look upon themselves as belonging to the same *society,* or *community,* as the Gentry; but who ought always to be 'kept down in their proper place'. And it has become, of late, the fashion to consider the labouring classes in England in the same light, and to speak of them and treat them accordingly, which never was the case in a former age.

Four years later, in an open letter 'to the stocking-weavers of Lancashire, Nottingham and Derby', then engaged in a dispute with their employers, Cobbett returned to the same theme:

What is the cause, the primary cause of all this turmoil: of all this unnatural strife between *masters* and *men*? For, I like the words a great deal better than the new fangled jargon of *Employer* and *Operative.* When *master* and *man*

The Wensleydale knitters

Basket-makers at work

were the terms, everyone was in his place and all were free. Now, . . . it is an affair of *masters* and *slaves* and the word, master, seems to be avoided only for the purpose of covering our shame.

Cobbett attributed such changes largely to a particular adversary of his, 'Parson' Malthus, 'who considers men as *mere animals*'. It was due to Malthus, he felt, that 'we now frequently hear the working classes called "the population", just as we call the animals upon a farm, "the stock" ', the implication being, of course, that they existed solely for their owner's profit. Malthus certainly encouraged the notion that, as the whole survival of the nation depended upon discouraging the poor from acquiring families they could not support, it was almost an employer's duty not to give his men more than they needed for mere subsistence. But there were other factors at

work, too. While a village, where the occupants would be personally known at least to their employers, was often said to consist of a certain number of souls, a factory-owner referred to the men and women on his pay-roll as hands. Both farmer and factory-owner agreed that their work-people's role in life was to labour for their master's profit until they could work no more, but, with rare exceptions like Robert Owen or the Fieldens, the paternalism which existed in the countryside was lacking in the town.

Although 'the drift from the land' was a phenomenon which much exercised observers throughout the nineteenth century, by 1811 it had not in fact made much progress. The real progress of industrialisation and the major population explosion in the towns of the North and Midlands was yet to come. Already, however, the number of families in England, Wales and Scotland engaged in 'trade, manufacture or handicraft', i.e. all industrial and commercial occupations, (1,129,000) substantially exceeded those 'chiefly employed in agriculture' (896,000), the remainder (519,000 families) including all others—land-owners, professional people other than business-men, and those of independent means. In percentage terms the breakdown was 44% in trade, 35% in agriculture and 21% in neither. By 1831 the picture was changing, but not very markedly.

Whether the life of a factory-worker was worse than that of a farm labourer must remain a matter of opinion. The former was usually at least warm and dry and he was almost certainly better fed, clothed and housed, although owing to the unhealthiness of urban life, his expectation of life was less. As Chadwick pointed out in his classic Report on the *Sanitary Condition of the*

Labouring Population a generation later, in 1842, a Leicestershire farm-hand could expect to live twice as long as a Manchester mechanic, and a farmer to survive a city grocer born at the same time. The fact that many farm labourers 'voted with their feet' and left the land during the early nineteenth century suggests that the horrors of factory life may well have been exaggerated, at least by contrast with the continuing misery and servitude of life on the land. Nor can factory life conceivably have been much worse than that of people engaged in industrial processes in their own homes, like the chain-makers of the Black Country, who spent their whole lives surrounded by the dirt and noise of a factory in miniature. Long before the end of the century 'out-work', looked back to so nostalgically in the 1820s and the 1830s, was regarded as almost inseparable from squalor and sweated labour.

There were exceptions, notably the hand-loom weavers, the aristocrats among out-workers, who were enjoying a temporary prosperity due to the introduction of machine-spinning. Most such men owned, or rented, one or two looms, and whose relationship with the small 'masters' who employed them was one of friendly informality, and sturdy independence. The future Radical leader, Samuel Bamford, who had been born at Middleton in Lancashire in 1788, worked as a boy alongside his uncle, who made handkerchiefs and 'occasionally . . . silk and cotton garments', for a Manchester firm, witnessed the closing stages of this happy era in the decade before 1810:

The family were at that time chiefly employed by Messrs Samuel and James Broadbent, of Cannon Street (Manchester) . . .
    We mounted some steps, went along a covered passage, and up a height or two of stairs, to a

Silk weaving

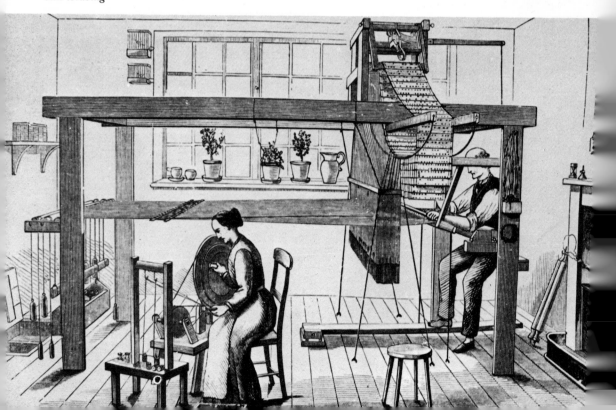

landing place, one side of which was . . .
furnished with a seat for weavers to rest upon
when they arrived. Here we should probably find
some half dozen weavers and winders, waiting
for their turn to deliver in their work and
receive fresh material: and the business betwixt
workman and putter-out was generally done in an
amicable, reasonable way. No captious fault-
finding, no bullying, no arbitrary abatement,
which have been too common since. . . . If the
work were really faulty, the weaver was shewn
the fault and if it were not a serious one he was
only cautioned against repeating it; if the length
or the weight was not what it should be, he was
told of it, and would be expected to set it right
or account for it, at his next bearing home. . . .
But very rarely indeed did it happen that any
transaction bearing the appearance of an
advantage being taken against the workman by
the putter out was heard of in those days.

Already, complained Bamford, things had,
in the opinion of the older men, 'greatly
altered for the worse'.

Market Street, Manchester

The two classes of workmen were already at too
great a distance from each other and it was a
subject of observation that the masters were
becoming more proud and uplifted each day. . . .
Some weavers had seen the time, when, on the
taking their work home, and material not being
ready . . . master and man would walk together
to some decent looking house, in some decent,
quiet street, where the master, his wife, his
children, and the guest, would sit down to a plain
substantial dinner of broth, most likely, with
dumpling and meat, or roast beef and baked
pudding, or a steaming potatoe pie: after
which, master and workman would sit with their
ale and pipes, talking about whatever most
concerned themselves . . . the lady of the house
also being present with her knitting.

Now, however, if they had to wait, the men
went off on their own, Bamford's uncle,
like other weavers, favouring *'The Hope and
Anchor* in the Old Church yard . . . where
we lunched on bread and cheese, or cold
meat and bread, with ale'.

But life was still pleasant enough, even if one makes allowance for the patina of nostalgia added by time:

The 'bearing home wallet' was often both bulky and heavy: and, when it happened to be too much for one person to carry, a neighbour's wallet would be borrowed, the burden divided into two, and I would go with one part over my shoulder, behind or before my uncle. He . . . would walk deliberately with a stick in his hand, his green woollen apron twisted round his waist, his clean shirt showing at the open breast of his waistcoat, his brown silk handkerchief wrapped round his neck, a quid of tobacco in his mouth, and a broad and rather slouched hat on his head. . . . I, with my smaller wallet . . . my rough jacket, my knee breeches, my strong stockings and shoes, my open collared shirt, and pleasure and glee in my heart and countenance, footed the way as lightsomely as a young colt. . . .

Even apart from these excursions, life for the weavers of Middleton was remarkably different from the factory dominated existence soon to succeed it. There were traditional holidays, with accompanying rituals, for most seasons of the year. At Christmas, 'the ale was tapped, the currant loaf was sliced out', if the weather was fine and cold there was 'sliding' if wet 'a swinging rope in the loom-house', the day ending 'by assembling in parties of a dozen or a score', around someone's fireside. The celebration of 'the night of the first of May' (i.e. the early hours of May morning) still had a bucolic, even pastoral quality about it. A holly-bush outside someone's door meant a secret admirer, a spray of birch was the young men's tribute to a pretty girl, while 'a gorse bush indicated a woman notoriously immodest'. It is hard indeed to imagine such harmless, centuries-old, rituals still surviving even a decade later. On May Morning, as on any other, the first factory generation clattered in their clogs towards

Riding the 'Stang'—a punishment for quarrelsome or licentious conduct

Four English Radicals
Samuel Bamford

William Cobbett

William Lovett

Francis Place

the mill at the summons of the clanging bell which ruled their lives.

Although Bamford considered 'the mode of living at my uncles was of the simplest country style' it, too, would have seemed even a little later remarkably luxurious. The family had porridge with milk and 'a piece of hard oaten cake' with 'a little butter or a small piece of cheese' for breakfast, followed by, 'butcher's meat and potatoes, or potato-pie, or meat and broth or barm [i.e. yeast] dumplings, or . . . hasty pudding' for their dinner. Later, at what is now tea-time, was 'bagging, or afternoon lunch', which 'consisted of half an oaten cake, with butter, treacle, cheese or milk . . . and our supper was generally the same as breakfast'. The highlights of the dietary week came on Sunday with 'mint tea' and, in the afternoon, 'a slice of buttered loaf, . . . as an especial dainty'.

Bamford was not the only weaver to look back on this period as a golden age before the machines arrived to rob this peaceful and contented community—or so it seemed in retrospect—of its whole way of life. A former handloom weaver from Manchester, James Brennan, who gave evidence to a Select Committee of the House of Commons in 1834, also recalled his early years—he had entered the trade in 1811—as a time of almost unimaginable affluence. Although 'but a boy' he could, he testified, 'earn 12s per week then', or nine shillings after expenses, while now, as an experienced adult, his pay, after deductions, averaged only 7s 6d, and only the 5s a week his wife earned at a cotton mill kept the family

A Sheffield Street

afloat. 'As a young man' recalled Brennan, 'I . . . had three suits of clothes . . . a good watch in my pocket . . . two or three pair of shoes and one or two good hats'. Now he had only one new garment, his best trousers, bought twelve months before and put on that day for the Committee's benefit. His shoes he was buying by instalments, and his household "apparatus" he had inherited from his parents since 'I never had it in my power to buy any since I have been married'. Lacking decent clothing, he did not like to go to church and he could not afford to belong to a friendly society, so that if he fell ill, 'I have to work myself well again'. His sole luxury was to 'have all my children, my wife and myself, in a penny club for burial'.

Many other casualties of the Industrial Revolution were, however, in far worse case than this man. A survey made in 1836 covering thirty-five manufacturing townships which lived mainly on handloom weaving in Lancashire and Yorkshire and contained 203,000 people found that the average amount available for food and clothing, after payment of rent, was 1s 3¼d a week per head. One man who appeared before the House of Commons Committee agreed that, 'after making the minimum provision for necessities, such as was barely sufficient to keep him in existence' his income was actually 'minus 1s 4d to supply himself with . . . lodgings and proper food', the equation being balanced by his going ragged and hungry. Conditions in another formerly flourishing textile area, Lanarkshire, were no better. One man living

A Manchester Mill

near Motherwell told an investigator that 'tea, coffee, sugar, soap, ham and cheese are articles which, although formerly deemed essentials, are seldom seen upon a weaver's table', while another, in Airdrie, explained that despite 'the man and his apprentices toiling sixteen or eighteen hours a day', they ate only 'parritch [i.e. porridge] in the morning, and potatoes and salt to dinner and the same to supper, or sometimes a wee drap brose' [i.e. oatmeal porridge]. Their solitary luxury was 'a cup of tea . . . on Sabbath morning'.

The same observer also described the physical surroundings of 'the lower classes of inhabitants', anticipating by a decade Chadwick's great study:

The houses are of the most flimsy and imperfect construction. In a very few years they become ruinous to a degree. One of the circumstances in which they are especially defective is that of drainage and water-closets. Whole ranges of these houses are either totally undrained, or only very partially. . . . The whole of the washings and filth from these consequently are thrown into the front or back street, which being often unpaved and cut up into deep ruts allows them to collect into stinking and stagnant pools, while, fifty or more having only a single convenience common to them all, it is in a very short time completely choked up.

Many rows of houses in 'the manufacturing districts' the same critic found, were 'built back to back, fronting one way into a narrow court, across which the inmates of the opposite houses may shake hands without stepping out of their own doors; and the other way, into a back street, unpaved and unsewered'. Even excluding the Irish, who often lived in a damp cellar, shared with a pig, with 'a whole family . . . accommodated on a single bed', the home life of at least a large minority of the working class must at this time have been miserable indeed:

The houses of great numbers of labouring community in the manufacturing districts are filthy, unfurnished and deprived of all the accessories to decency or comfort. What little furniture is found in them is of the rudest and

Bethnal Green slums, 1863

most common sort, and very often in fragments—one or two rush-bottomed chairs, a deal table, a few stools, broken earthenware, such as dishes, tea-cups, etc., or more tin-kettles and cans, a few knives and forks; no fender, a bedstead or not, as the case may happen to be; blankets and sheets in the strict meaning of the words unknown—their place often being made up by sacking, a heap of flocks, or a bundle of straw, supplying the want of a proper bedstead and feather bed; and these cooped in a single room, which serves as a place for all domestic and household occupations.

Although there were clearly many exceptions, this was the home to which large numbers of operatives returned from the mills and factories. What of their lives there? Although some processes were innately exhausting, on the whole it was the hours, rather than the intensity of the work, which proved most fatiguing. In 1810, and for many years thereafter, the normal working day in that archtypal factory, a cotton mill, was from 5 a.m. to 7 p.m.

London slum

The average wage was about 10s, but this covered wide variations, from the 30s a week earned by the most skilled spinners of fine yarn through the young girl weavers, earning up to 16s, down to the nine year olds taking home 3s to 4s 6d. The long hours were dictated by economics; plant was costly and only paid for itself if worked more or less continuously, but night work was a rarity, and technological progress, which had first drawn the working class into the factories, also rapidly ameliorated their conditions inside them as one investigator, writing in 1836, discovered:

Subsequent to 1806, when the steam-loom was first brought into operation, many of the first mills were either much enlarged, or in very numerous examples abandoned . . . and in their stead large buildings were erected, fitted to receive, in addition to the spinning processes, a quantity of looms. The rooms were much more lofty, generally of large proportions, had numerous windows, so arranged as to afford

excellent ventilation. . . . The gradual substitution of iron in the frame-work of the machinery . . . by its diminished bulk materially increased the empty space in the rooms, the wooden frames having been large and massy. . . . Since steam-weaving became general, the number of adults engaged in the mills has been progressively advancing, inasmuch that very young children are not competent to take charge of a steam-loom.

If not quite as bad as legend has painted it, life in the early factories was still a grim strictly-disciplined, routine, as a pamphlet, issued on behalf of the spinners involved in a strike in a mill at Tyldesley, near Manchester, makes clear. 'At Tyldesley', protested the author, 'they work fourteen hours per day, including the nominal hour for dinner; the door is locked in working hours, except half an hour at teatime. . . . The work people are not allowed to send for water to drink, in the hot factory,' where the temperature reached 84 degrees. 'Even the rain water is locked up, by the master's order, otherwise they would be happy to drink even that'. The same pamphlet, reprinted in the *Political Register* in 1823, gave a list of the fines in operation in the same mill:

	s	d
Any spinner found with his window open	1	0
Any spinner leaving his oil can out of his place	1	0
Any spinner putting his gas out too soon	1	0
Any spinner spinning with gaslight too long in the morning	2	0
Any spinner heard whistling	1	0
Any spinner being five minutes after last bell rings	1	0
Any spinner being sick and cannot find another spinner to give satisfaction must pay for steam per day	6	0
Any spinner having a little waste on his spindles	1	0

Victorian stocking factory

RULES AND REGULATIONS
TO BE OBSERVED BY THE
WORKMEN
EMPLOYED BY
SAMUEL BASTOW,
CLIFF HOUSE IRON WORKS.

I.

The Engagement of each Workman shall be subject to a Fortnight's Notice, such Notice to be given at the Office on the pay day only, except in Cases of Dismissal for misconduct.

II.

Each Workman to enter and leave Work by the Office Door, where he must put his Ticket in the Box in the Morning, and at each Mealtime, or he will not have any time allowed for such neglect, the Box being open Five Minutes for that purpose, previous to the time of commencing Work; and in the Morning Five Minutes after the time for commencing Work.

III.

Any Workman absenting himself from his Employment for a longer period than 2 Working Days, without leave, shall be held to have left his service, and dealt with accordingly.

IV.

Work to commence at 6 o'clock in the Morning, and to end at 6 o'clock at Night, except on Saturdays, when the Days Work shall end at 4 o'clock, and on the Pay Saturday at 2 o'clock, no Dinner hour being allowed.

V.

Meal Hours to be from 8 to ½ past 8 o'clock, for Breakfast; and 12 to 1 o'clock, for Dinner. No Dinner Hour being allowed on Pay Saturdays.

VI.

Time to be kept by the *Hour.*—10 Working Hours to be a day's work.

VII.

The Door shall be closed every Morning when the Bell Rings, at 6 o'clock; but, should any Workman over-sleep himself, he may be admitted at 10 minutes past 6 o'clock, forfeiting ¼ an hour.

VIII.

When required, every Workman shall Work overtime.—Such overtime being paid for at and after the rate of 8 Working hours to a day's Work, but no overtime to be reckoned until full time has been Worked.

IX.

Workmen employed at out door Work, to be subject to the same time as in the Shop, except during the months of November, December, and January, when the Day's work shall commence at Day Light, and end at Dark,—no time being allowed for Breakfast. When Working at a greater Distance than Three Miles, to be paid 2s. per, week for Lodgings.

X.

Workmen employed at the Marine Engine Work, or at Boats in either Harbour, to commence and end Work the same as in the Works.

XI.

Every Workman to be accountable for his Tools, and in case of loss or injury, the amount to be deducted from his wages.

XII.

Wages to be paid every alternate Saturday, and the time made up Fortnightly, to the previous Thursday Night.

XIII.

The time worked after the Thursday Night, on the Pay Week, to be Lying Time; and in any case where less than two Lying Days have been worked, the difference shall be kept in hand out of the Wages due.

XIV.

Any Workman absenting himself, without leave, during Work Hours, or after commencing his Day's Work, to forfeit the Wages earned on that day, and to pay a fine of 2s. 6d.

XV.

Any Workman making pr﹘ ﹘eave his Work, before the Bell Ring﹘, ﹘o pay a Fine of 2s. 6d. men,—and 1s. boys.

XVI.

Any Workman found in any other part of the Works than where his Work requires him, to pay 1s. for the first, and 2s. 6d. for the second offence.

XVII.

Workmen requiring New Tools, or their Old ones dressed, or exchanged, shall not remain at the Smithy, Store House, or other place, after giving the necessary instructions; if found at any of these places after such instructions HAVE BEEN GIVEN, to forfeit 2s. 6d. NEW Files will not be given out except in exchange FOR THOSE WORN OUT.

XVIII.

Any Workman Smoking during Work Hours, or seen on the Premises the worse for Liquor, to pay a fine of 5s., or to be dismissed at the option of his Employers.

XIX.

Any one bringing Spirits into the Works, to pay a fine of 5s., or to be dismissed at the option of his Employers.

XX.

Any one refusing to obey the orders of his Foreman, or using insolent and abusing language to any one in charge, or quarrelling with his Fellow-workman, to pay a fine of 5s., or to be dismissed at the option of his Employer.

XXI.

Any one using Oil, Waste, or other Article, for improper purposes; leaving Candles burning; neglecting to turn off his Gas Burner; taking Strangers into the Works without leave; or talking to Strangers in the Works, to pay a fine of 2s. 6d.

XXII.

Any one engaged in the Works, taking Dimensions or Copies of Drawings, will be discharged.

XXIII.

Any workman taking another's Tools, or neglecting to return Taps and Dies, or any general Tool, to the Persons in charge of them, to pay a fine of 2s. 6d. And any workman injuring any Machinery or Tool, or defacing Drawings, Plans, or Copies of these Rules, to be fined 5s.

XXIV.

Any Workman breaking windows, either wilfully or from carelessness, to pay for repairing same.

NOTE.—Apprentices to be subject to these Rules, but without prejudice to their Indentures.

All Fines will be strictly enforced, and the Amount applied to the Benefit of the Sick Club.

HARTLEPOOL: J. PROCTER, PRINTER, AND LITHOGRAPHER, HIGH STREET.

Although some such regulations were reasonable, and may even have been safety precautions, like one penalising any operative 'repairing his drum banding with his gas lighted', the overall impression they created was of a regime in which personality, and even dignity, were lost. The real taskmaster now was the machine, as one writer pointed out in 1836:

The labourer is indeed become a subsidiary to this power. Already he is condemned, hour after hour, day after day, to watch and minister to its operations—to become himself as much a part of its mechanism as its cranks and cog-wheels—already to feel that he is but a portion of a mighty machine, very improved application of which . . . every addition to its . . . arms, rapidly lessens his importance, and tend to drive him from a participation with it, as the most expensive and unmanageable part of its materials.

A survey of wages throughout the United Kingdom in 1810 and later years reveals some large regional variations, with wages in Glasgow usually, though not invariably, from 1s to 5s lower than those paid in Manchester or Bolton. At the very top of the scale, inevitably, were the compositors on London morning newspapers, earning £2 8s a week, an income which many a curate or governess would have envied. At the very bottom, equally inevitably, were labourers, both urban and rural, earning in Manchester 15s a week, in Glasgow 11s, with farm workers (except in a few particularly ill-paid counties) averaging 13s a week. In between came tradesmen of varying degrees of skill: Carpenters: 25s a week in Manchester, 18s in Glasgow; Bricklayers: 22s 6d and 17s; Masons: 22s and 17s; Tailors: 18s 6d in Manchester, and, unusually, 6d more in Glasgow; Shoemakers: 16s and 15s and—already a special case, slipping down the earnings table—hand-loom weavers 16s 3d in Manchester, 11s 6d in Glasgow. Another survey adds additional trades such as miners, earning in Scotland 5s a day, and ironmoulders, high up the table with 31s a week. The earnings of the 'mule-spinners', using one of the earliest inventions to transform the cotton industry, Samuel Crompton's 'mule' which produced a finer and stronger thread than hand spinning, thus making possible the production of high quality muslin, at 25s–30s a week, showed clearly enough that machinery was by no means a threat to the livelihood of those who learned to master it. Engineers, a trade barely known twenty years earlier, already earned 28s a week, another portent of changes still to come. With the exception of the hand-loom weavers, most of these rates of pay altered little during the following twenty years, apart from minor variations due to the state of trade. The pattern of occupations however, changed markedly during this period. The cotton industry, with only 162,000 employees in 1787 was by 1831 one of the two or three largest in the country, with 833,000.

It is often forgotten that it was not only brutal employers who were responsible for child labour (though workhouse children whom no-one wanted were its worst victims) but parents who, with varying degrees of reluctance, put their children into the mills. A child's earnings could make all the difference between hardship and comparative comfort for a family as figures collected for a number of cotton trade families in 1811 make clear. The best-off, a fine spinner, earning 18s 0d, could count on another 4s 0d from a child aged fourteen and 1s 6d from one aged ten, raising his total income to 23s 6d. At the middle of the scale, the children's earnings were the same, but their father, a male weaver, earned only 9s 6d, giving them a total income of 15s od. At the bottom of the scale the children's earnings became vital to survival, accounting for 5s 6d of the 13s 11d coming in, their mother, a stretcher, earning no more herself than 8s 5d. These figures compare with estimates of the cost of feeding a rather larger family, of six people, at the same time. A reasonable diet, including a certain amount of meat, bacon, butter, cheese, treacle and sugar, as well as the duller necessities like flour, oatmeal and potatoes, required a weekly expenditure of just under 15s 6d, easily attained by the most prosperous but clearly beyond the reach of the worst-paid.

In 1836 a statement was published of the 'Proper Weekly Expenditure of a Man, Wife and Four Children', all of them aged under eight, based on 'the way weavers lived when I was one and trade was good', i.e. presumably around 1810. Though clearly much too lavish for the lower-paid, as the weavers themselves soon became, it probably reflects fairly accurately, if 'loom-rent' is omitted, the standard of living of the skilled artisan in regular employment in the first quarter of the nineteenth century:

Market for hiring children, 1850

	£	s	d
House rent: room and kitchen		1	6
Loom Rent		1	0
Fire			8
Candle or oil			6
Soap, 1 lb			8
Church seats, taxes, police money			4
Clothing, including shirts, stockings, etc.		3	3
Shoes		1	3
		9	2

Food

One peck of oatmeal for bread		1	0
Two pecks of oatmeal for breakfast and supper to children		2	0
Two oz of tea for breakfast			9
1 lb of butter		1	3
Loaf bread (i.e. not home-baked)		1	0
1 lb sugar			7
Ham, fish or cheese		1	2
Milk		1	0
Butcher's meat, 8 lb		3	4
Barley			8
Potatoes and other vegetables		1	0
		13	9
TOTAL	1	2	11

Such a budget required an income which many families would have envied a century later, but the hand-loom weavers' position was to change spectacularly, his earnings dropping from an average 18s a week—though many, like the one just quoted, made substantially more—to no more than 6s 3d by 1830. 'The hand-loom weavers', wrote the author of *The Manufacturing and Physical Conditions of the Manufacturing Population* in 1836, had been 'crushed by their mighty opponent', the steam engine, 'into the dust'. For most of the working population, however, the very reverse had happened. Thanks to powered machinery 'the labourer, though losing rapidly his independent character, is paid for his labour a sum amply sufficient, when properly applied, to supply all his natural wants and to provide him with comforts and opportunities for making provision for sickness or old age, without becoming a burden upon the fixed capital of the nation'.

If he did not eat as well as the weaver just described had done a quarter of a century before the factory worker in the 1830s rarely went hungry. 'The staple diet of the town-mill artisan', wrote the same observer, 'is potatoes and wheaten bread, washed down by tea or coffee. Milk is little used. Meal is consumed to some extent, either baked into cakes or boiled up with water, making a porridge at once nutritious, easy of digestion and readily cooked. Herrings are eaten not unusually. . . . Eggs, too, form some portion of the operative's diet. The staple, however, is tea and bread'. Butcher's meat was rarely included except on the table of fine spinners and others, 'whose wages are very liberal', but all sections of the working class, except the very poorest, tended by the 1830s to consider tea and sugar, once near-luxuries, as necessities. Between 1814 and 1832 the population rose by 24%, while the 'amount of sugar consumed' went up 83% and of tea by 65%.

But what had happened since 1810 was not all gain:

The mode of life which the system of labour pursued in manufactories forces upon the operative, is one singularly unfavourable to domesticity. Rising at or before day-break, between four and five o'clock the year round, he swallows a hasty meal, or hurries to the mill without taking any food whatever. At eight o'clock half an hour, and in some instances, forty minutes, are allowed for breakfast. In many cases, the engine continues at work . . . obliging the labourer to eat and still overlook his work. . . . This meal is brought to the mill, and generally consists of weak tea, of course nearly cold, with a little bread; in other instances, of milk-and-meal porridge. Tea, however, may be called the universal breakfast, flavoured of late years too often with gin or other stimulants.

At twelve o'clock the engine stops and an hour is given for dinner. The hands leave the mill and seek their homes, where this meal is usually taken. It consists of potatoes boiled, very often eaten alone; sometimes with a little bacon and sometimes with a portion of animal food (i.e. meat). This latter is, however, only food at the tables of the more provident and reputable workmen. If, as it often happens, the majority of the labourers reside at some distance, a great portion of the allotted time is necessarily taken up by the walk, or rather run, backwards and forwards. No time is allowed for the observance of ceremony. The meal has been imperfectly cooked, by someone left for that purpose, not unusually a mere child, or superannuated man or woman. The entire family surround the table, if they possess one, each striving which can most rapidly devour the fare before them, which is sufficiently by its quantity to satisfy the cravings of hunger, but possesses little nutritive quality. . . . As soon as this is effected the family is again scattered. No rest has been taken and so even the exercise, such as it is, is useless from its excess and even harmful, being taken at a time when repose is necessary for the digestive operations. Again they are engaged from one o'clock till eight or nine, with the exception of twenty minutes, this being allowed for tea, or baggin-time as it is called. This imperfect meal is almost universally taken in the mill; it consists of tea and wheaten bread, with very few exceptions. . . . It must be remembered that father, mother, son and daughter are alike engaged; no one capable of working is spared to make home comfortable and desirable. No clean and tidy wife appears to welcome her husband—no smiling and affectionate mother to receive her children—no home, cheerful and inviting, to make it regarded. On the contrary it is badly furnished—dirty and squalid in its appearance.

With such a long working day most people were too tired to enjoy their scanty leisure and the commonest recreation was drinking, not necessarily, as the temperance reformers, active in this period, liked to suggest, a brainless soaking, but often a sociable gathering in a place more spacious and better furnished than the average working class home. Public-houses seemed to spring up in newly-built districts that lacked all other communal buildings,—even churches (as pious evangelicals were soon pointing out); after 1830, when the Beer Act simplified the licensing procedure, almost any dwelling house could sell beer and cider. Some men undoubtedly drank to escape from the drudgery of their lives and the squalor of their environment. 'The quickest way out of Ancoats' ran the famous saying about one particularly squalid part of Manchester, 'is through the public house door'.

The 'pub' was already the great centre of working class social life. In the four, out of fourteen, districts of Manchester which in 1836 'belonged exclusively to the labouring population', there were '270 taverns, 216 gin shops and 188 beer houses', total 674. One city official, who carried out a private census of the patronage of one of these establishments on eight successive Saturday nights in 1832–3 found that in forty minutes it was visited by 112 men and 163 women, a rate of custom of 412 people per hour.

Later in the century, trade union leaders and radical politicians were frequently militant teetotallers—a word not coined until 1832—and many union rule-books then included a ban on holding meetings in public houses, while by the 1870s the hysterical hostility of the 'waterdrinking' wing of the Liberal Party had driven the licensed trade into being solidly Conservative. But in earlier decades licensees were often men of progressive views and the infant working-class movement would have fared hard without their cooperation in making rooms available as meeting-places for union meetings and turning a blind eye to what went on there.

The role of the public house in working class life was crucial in other ways too. Until well on into the 1830s gangs of labourers, or all the men in a workshop, might be paid there, a single banknote being given to one man who relied on the publican to change it, his commission being the drinks immediately bought from it. Certain pubs served, too, as informal labour exchanges, to which a man seeking work automatically applied, and in riverside areas of London the licensee was often the contractor who provided casual dockside labour. Many pubs also served as the unofficial headquarters of all those working locally in a particular craft, and names like *The Jolly Carpenters* or *The Masons' Arms* originally advertised such connections. It was understood in many trades that a man 'on the tramp' in search of work had only to call at the appropriate pub to have food and shelter provided and perhaps be given a donation, sometimes on a fixed scale, to help him on his way.

The origins of trade unionism already lay, around 1810, in the distant past, in the craft guilds of the Middle Ages, but trade unions in a more modern sense only began in the eighteenth century. These early combinations, to use the contemporary

word, took two forms: groups of workers joining briefly together to air a particular grievance or make some specific demand on the employer, and more permanent organisations, usually confined to the members of a single workshop, or those practising the same craft in a single area, striving to protect their long-term interests, especially by controlling admission to their own trade. On the fringes of the movement were the Friendly Societies and Sick Clubs which provided the poor man's only real protection against unemployment and illness, promising him maintenance when he needed it, and other benefits such as a 'lying-in' allowance for his wife, medical attendance and a funeral grant, in return for a small weekly contribution.

In 1799 it became illegal, under the Combination Acts, for any workman to join with others to try to secure an increase in wages, a decrease in hours or any improvement in his conditions of service. This meant in practice that one broke the law not only by organising but even by belonging to a union, though a society serving purely social purposes could still exist and there was no restriction on the freedom of employers to act together. The Combination Acts were prompted by a petition to the House of Commons from a group of employers pleading for protection against 'a dangerous combination . . . among the journeyman millwrights within the metropolis . . . and twenty-five miles round . . . for enforcing a general increase of their wages', though underlying them, and their ready acceptance by M.P.s, lay the almost universal fear of revolutionary influences spreading from France. Under the Acts anyone who attended a meeting to raise wages, or tried to collect money for union purposes, could be sent summarily to jail

for three months, while a sympathiser who attempted to raise money to finance an appeal against conviction was liable to a £10 fine. An individual holding trade union funds was required to surrender them and betray the contributors, and could be convicted merely for refusing to give evidence which might incriminate himself. The Acts ushered in what one contemporary described as 'the English Age of Terror', but this was an exaggeration. By continental standards they were very mild and proved in any case singularly ineffective. The reports reaching the Home Office revealed that unions continued to exist and help each other in many parts of the country, and for every letter intercepted there must have been many more undetected. The fainter hearts perhaps fell away but persecution only made the 'real union men' more determined, like this Liverpool shoemaker, whose letter to colleagues in another town, ended up in Whitehall:

Loving shopmaites,

I hope you will excuse our neglect in not wrighting before now to return to you our grateful thanks for your timley assistance in our last contest with the tyrant. . . . We still and allways shall think our indeted to you for the suploys we receive from you without wich we must have suffered verray much . . . for we have so maney disarters. . . . Amongst disarters . . . John Welch and Thomas Richards and all the others has reduced thare wages 2 pence pr paire wich we hope you will make as publick through your meetings what villands we have had amongst us. . . . At the request of Mr. Richardshon our seckeretarey I was to inform you of the coduct of Charles Duggeon wo with 2 others dubblin bootmen has gone to our tyrant phillipps a longue with the other scabbs. . . .

I remain your truley
in defence of the traide
F. Capper.

Union activity also continued not merely among such notoriously recalcitrant groups as the textile workers of Bolton and the cotton weavers of Salford—Industrial Lancashire, the birthplace and heartland of the Industrial Revolution, was often assumed in Whitehall at this time to be on the brink of revolution—but among less powerful groups such as the paper makers of Surrey and Sussex and the journeyman tailors and bakers of the capital. A surviving letter from the paper-makers reports that, unawed by the Combination Acts, the branch concerned had raised 'our fifth subscription of 2s 6d each, which makes 12s 6d per man', and refers to a meeting of 'a very respectable body of our trade, forty-four in number, where I produced the sick and secret articles of our trade which were generally and universally approved and signed and are to be printed; also the cards of freedom', presumably membership cards. The writer concluded with a stirring prediction: 'Manchester and Wells approve of our plan and they say they will establish it in every mill from Berwick to Lands End'.

Such experiences, though largely confined to the small craft unions where combination was easiest, were not exceptional and there was a good deal of mutual help between unions during the years of repression. One small society, the London Goldbeaters, sent sums of money ranging from £5 to £30 to help eight other unions, during 1810 alone. Most of it went to allied trades, such as the silversmiths, the braziers and the bookbinders, but there were also loans to 'ye brushmakers . . . ye bit and spurmakers' and 'ye ropemakers' whose connection with gold-beating was obscure. Some unions, or groups of workmen, also managed during this period to keep up the fight for a 'closed shop' nominally to maintain standards or workmanship but in practice to increase its members' value and make it easier to maintain restrictive practices, a constant aim in the history of many trades. The future Radical campaigner William Lovett, arriving in London in 1821 from Penzance, where he had served an apprenticeship as a rope-maker, was soon at odds with his workmates in a cabinet workshop, who, learning he came from outside their trade, threatened to 'set Mother Thorney' at him, which meant driving him out by stealing his tools, damaging his work, and general bullying. But Lovett already had in him the stuff of a radical orator and called a meeting of his tormentors, when his eloquent explanation, aided by a gallon of ale, led to his being allowed to stay. Often thereafter, however, he had to pay other men 'fines' for being shown a particular process, deductions which sometimes added up to eight shillings out of the twenty-one he earned each week. Later, as president of the Cabinet-Makers Society, Lovett himself became a rigorous enforcer of its closed-shop policy.

The closed shop principle illustrates well the different points of view of employer and employee. The men argued that, having, over long years' of experience, mastered a trade, they were entitled to charge a new entrant for teaching it to him—an argument that possessed some force when there was no

Casting a cylinder for a bridge

systematic technical training outside provided by the community—or the newcomer to the workshop for allowing him in to their little fraternity. The workman, as was so often said later, had nothing to sell but his labour and his skill. Why, he argued, should he not market them as sparingly as possible on the best terms he could exact, just as his employer did with his products?

Despite the Combination Acts the closed-shop survived unaffected where it already existed, providing a nucleus for future union growth, but the Acts did have two unforeseen effects. One was a marked expansion of the Friendly Societies, which remained legal, and their membership increased from about 700,000 in 1803 to 925,000 in 1815, though they mainly remained small, and often local, organisations, whose principal non-insurance activities were purely social, such as annual outings and dinners. The societies however, often made a positive fetish of secrecy, with elaborate admission ceremonies and private rituals—procedures soon to be turned to less innocent purposes. The other result of the war on the unions was to create the very type of conspiracy the Combination Acts were designed to root out. Many working men's fraternities, instead of being open in their aims and methods, now became secret, protecting their membership by fearsome oaths and ready to resort to violence, not merely against employers but against any of their workmates

Messrs Marshall's Flax Mill—factory hands leaving for dinner

who failed to support them. This threat of force underlay many disputes throughout the nineteenth century and inevitably flourished most in the secret years from 1799 when the Combination Acts were in force.

In Newcastle in 1810 miners were required to swear their allegiance to a strike, and to instant obedience to their leaders, under penalty of 'being stabbed through the heart or of having their bowels ripped up' and even if not to be taken literally, any more than the comparable pledges entered into by freemasons, such threats were not by any means mere rhetoric. 'Blacklegs', or men who refused to join a union, or a strike, were often bullied or assaulted and one Glasgow cotton manufacturer reported to the Home Secretary in 1823 that the union there was so powerful that 'not only the masters but the industrious workmen must obey its orders . . . if they wished to avoid being murdered or excoriated with vitriol'.

Even while combinations were still illegal, and working men could be, and not infrequently were, charged with other offences, such as conspiracy and administering illegal oaths, arising from trade union activities, some men dreamed of vast federations in which working men from all over the country would work together to demand their rights. In 1818 representatives of a dozen trades actually

assembled in Manchester to found the Philanthropic Hercules for the Mutual Support of the Labouring Classes but its name proved more heroic than its achievements and it came to nothing. That vast uprising of the 'productive classes'—as Robert Owen, a little later, described them—which the authorities dreaded was never either feasible or contemplated, except by a few near lunatic hotheads, and with Napoleon safe on St Helena and the Bourbons restored in France some of the original fears receded.

In 1824 the Combination Acts were repealed, thus making trade unionism legal once more, and ten years later, in 1834, there was an attempt to form a giant, national federation, embracing many different crafts, in the Grand National Consolidated Trades Union, which reflected the ideas of Robert Owen, and soon acquired a million members, more than the whole parliamentary electorate at that time, only to outgrow its strength and collapse. For many years to come trade unionism was to remain both 'vertically' divided also, with the societies in various parts of the country having little contact with each other and bargaining independently.

LANCASHIRE

● Rawdon

● **LEEDS**

Gildersome
● **HALIFAX** ● Rawfolds

HUDDERSFIELD ●

● Horbury

● Westhoughton

Middleton ●

MANCHESTER ●

YORKSHIRE

STOCKPORT ●

CHESHIRE

DERBYSHIRE

● Mansfield

Alfreton ● Sutton-in-Ashfield
Crich ● ● Blidworth
Ripley ● Kirkby-in-Ashfield
Heanor ● Eastwood
Kimberley ● Redhill
Ilkeston ● ● Bulwell Arnold ● Lowdham
Stapleford ● **NOTTINGHAM** ● Burton Joyce
Long Eaton ● ● Beeston
Chilwell
Castle Donington ● Ruddington
Melbourne ● ● Kegworth

Shepshed ● ● Loughborough

**LOCATIONS OF MACHINE-BREAKING
IN SIX COUNTIES 1811-16**

LEICESTERSHIRE

● **LEICESTER**

2 Three cheers for General Ludd

Those engines of mischief were sentenced to die
By unanimous vote of the trade.
And Ludd who can all opposition defy
Was the grand executioner made.
General Ludd's Triumph. c. 1812

Who was the original King Ludd, or
General Ludd, or Ned Ludd, as he was
variously known? According to one account
he was 'a youth named Ludlam, a reckless
character who, when his father, a frame-
work knitter, told him one day to "square
his needles" squared them effectually by
taking up his hammer and beating them into
a heap'. Another candidate, mentioned by
the *Nottingham Review* in December 1811,
was an apprentice frame-work knitter from
Anstey, near Leicester, genuinely called Ned
Ludd, who about 1782 was said to have been
ordered a whipping by the magistrate after
his master had complained that he was
'averse to work. . . . In answer [he] took a
hammer and demolished the hated frame'.
Whatever its origins, the name rapidly
passed into the folk-lore of the Midlands,
and wherever machinery was broken it was
said that 'Ned Ludd had passed that way'.
The name became a convenient cover for
any local leader and a useful signature to
threatening anonymous letters.

By the second decade of the nineteenth
century machine-breaking already had a
long ancestry, and on many occasions
during the eighteenth century not merely
were machines attacked but also raw
materials or the employer's private
property. The aim, however, was not to
prevent change, but, to quote one authority,
'collective bargaining by riot', i.e. to
terrorise an employer into coming to terms.
The Luddites differed from their
predecessors less in their methods than in
their motivation and the first manifestations
of what might be described as machine-
breaking as an end in itself occurred not
in the North, usually the most turbulent
part of the country, but in the traditionally
docile West. In 1797 several hundred men
had broken into a workshop grinding
mechanical shears near Frome in Somerset
and done thirty pounds worth of damage to
them, one of many such incidents. Yorkshire
experience some similar trouble at the
time and only escaped more because the
manufacturers and local authorities took the
line of least resistance. 'I have . . .', wrote
the mayor of Leeds in 1802, 'privately
prevailed upon one or two houses who
meditated the adding of a gigmill or a
shearing machine to their works to desist for
the present, or I am firmly convinced we
should have had such horrid outrages . . . as
have been practised in the West'. The
clothworkers around Leeds had by now
formed themselves into a closed shop, 'the
Institution', nominally a sick club. But it
was not in cloth manufacture but stocking-

making that the first real trouble occurred. This was still around 1810 little more than a cottage industry, with most of the 'masters' owning small workshops containing no more than three or four frames which they worked themselves. There were perhaps 50,000 workers employed in the trade, with some 30,000 looms between them, almost all in the areas around Nottingham and Leicester though the latter was a centre of finer quality work less affected by mechanisation.

Although taking place very much 'off stage' so far as the ordinary working man was concerned, the Napoleonic Wars, in which Britain was involved between 1793 and 1802 and again from 1803 until final victory in 1815, added to the prevailing unrest, not merely upsetting the normal pattern of trade but giving a tremendous impetus to radical doctrines. The war, far from uniting the country against a foreign enemy, was unpopular. There was little active opposition, but if there were few Bonapartists in the Midlands and the 'textile belt' of Lancashire and Yorkshire, there were certainly many 'Tom Painers' steeped in the doctrines of *The Rights of Man*. The driving force behind the Luddite movement was, however, in the true sense of the word, reactionary not revolutionary. A few men may have wished to go forward to a new and happier world, but the vast majority sought only to return to the security of the old one. Between 1800 and 1810 several unsuccessful petitions were addressed by textile workers to Parliament protesting that the introduction of machinery was an infringement of their traditional rights and pleading for protection against it.

As trade fell off the larger manufacturers in the hosiery trade anxious to economise, welcomed new types of loom. A writer in

The Examiner, in September 1812, described the result:

Those large engines for weaving produce *entire webbs* instead of a single stocking, as was formerly made from a frame, and the stockings from thence were cut out in pieces and sewed, resembling those goods woven upon the old stocking frames. A new kind of cheap lace was also made from larger frames by which labour was greatly diminished. The workmen who were before badly supplied with either labour or money, were now reduced to the most abject stage of misery.

Mingled with that most basic of motives, hunger,—in 1812 wheat reached the highest price on record—among the Nottingham stockingers (also known as framework-knitters), was, so some of them claimed, a desire to protect the reputation of their craft. A feature of the work turned out by the

Caricature of King Ludd

large looms just described was that some pieces known as 'cut-ups', because they were cut out of larger pieces of cloth and then sewn together, were of poorer quality than goods made in the traditional way. At first sight they resembled the genuine article, except in price, and the stocking-makers contended that they were giving the whole trade a bad name. 'The machines', claimed the *Nottingham Review*, 'are not broken for being upon any new construction . . . but in consequence of goods being wrought upon them which are of little worth, are deceptive to the eye, are disreputable to the trade, and therefore pregnant with the seeds of its destruction'. 'Cut-ups' posed, too, another threat to the older, skilled workmen. To produce them, and to man the new machines, required only comparatively unskilled labour, and, the journeymen contended, too many apprentices, or other unskilled recruits, were being brought into the trade, lowering its status and—what was in the long run clearly worse—vastly reducing the craftsmen's bargaining power. The movement against 'cut-ups' and 'colting', as employing too many recent recruits was known, was essentially one of the skilled men opposing the unskilled, but it was not exclusively one of workmen against masters. Many owners of the older types of frame, perhaps unable or unwilling to replace them, sympathised, at least in secret, with their men. Nor was Luddism, except almost by accident, a political movement; The song *General Ludd's Triumph* neatly set out the movement's aims in Nottingham, the first of the centres where it established itself:

The guilty may fear, but no vengeance he aims
At the honest man's life or estate.
His wrath is entirely confined to wide frames
And to those that old prices abate.
Those engines of mischief were sentenced to die

By unanimous vote of the trade,
And Ludd, who can all opposition defy,
was the grand executioner made.

'General Ludd first erected his standard', according to *The Examiner*, on the 11th March 1811, when, as a result of rising prices and falling wages, there were a series of strikes around Nottingham, culminating in a riot in the town. That night the crowd poured out of the city into the village of Arnold, where sixty stocking frames were smashed, the first of more than two hundred to be broken in the next three weeks. Soon attacks were occurring on several places in a single night, often by marauding parties divided into two, one standing guard while the other wrecked the machinery. Eventually four hundred special constables were enrolled, the local militia and volunteer yeomanry were called out and the disturbances ceased, only to break out again in the Autumn, on a more widespread and systematic basis, following the introduction by some hosiery-makers of a 'certain wide frame for the manufacture of stockings and garters . . . tending still farther to the decrease of the hands employed'. The *Leeds Mercury* for Saturday 23rd November 1811, reported the results:

On Sunday se'n night last (i.e. Sunday 10th November) a number of weavers assembled at different places in the vicinity of Nottingham and commenced their career of outrage by forcibly entering the houses of such persons as used particular frames. . . . A master weaver, at Bulwell, having been threatened by the rioters and hearing that they intended to attack his property, on the Monday armed all his men to defend his frames and barricaded his house. Being in his garrison, he waited the attack of the enemy, who demanded admittance, or a surrender of the frames. The master would agree to neither, and was immediately fired upon. Several shots were then exchanged, and one of the rioters was shot dead: he was a weaver from Arnold and at the time he was in the act of tearing down the window shutters to obtain entry by force.

The rest of the mob retired with the slain body, but soon returned with redoubled strength. They broke open the door and would have put the whole family to death had they not escaped by the back door. They then proceeded to gut the house, and consumed everything that would burn.

The funeral of this first Luddite martyr, a Leicester man called John Westley, led to an even more serious disturbance, as the *Leeds Mercury* duly recorded:

The scene was truly awful. From seven hundred to one thousand persons attended on the occasion. The corpse was preceded by a number of the deceased's former clubmates, bearing black wands, decked with knots of crepe. . . . The solemn silence . . . was only interrupted by the trampling of the multitude, the bell's heavy knoll and a band of music playing a solemn dirge, accompanied at distant intervals by the beating [of] a bass drum.

Later, however, the funereal solemnity was broken by the noise of an angry crowd, which rampaged through the streets until 'The Riot Act was read in several parts of the town'.[1] This was to be the pattern for many similar events elsewhere during the next few years.

On this occasion the soldiers proved effective. 'The riots at Nottingham', claimed the same newspaper on 28th November, 'have been partly put down by that powerful tranquilliser, a military force'. But the writer had rejoiced too soon. 'The depredations of the frame breakers are still continued', lamented another report only nine days later. 'Nor is the cause of this riotous condition confined to Nottingham— it exists in almost all the manufacturing districts of the Kingdom, both in woollens, cottons and iron, though Nottingham alone is happily the only scene of popular outrage'. Significantly, on both occasions the newspaper came close to expressing sympathy with the rioters. 'We wish', it wrote, referring to the suppression of the first riots, 'the same end had been accomplished by abundance of work and more liberal wages', while, of the spread of the trouble, it commented: 'To what an alarming crisis is this country brought when its military force, instead of being employed against our foreign enemies is obliged to act, reluctantly indeed, against our own subjects, made blind and desperate by privation and want'.

This reaction was typical. The Luddite struggles were not regarded by anyone at the time as a preliminary skirmish in a continuous class war. On the contrary, the aim of the men taking part was to restore the *status quo*. Nor were the aims of the Luddite movement political. The attribution of longer term, and nobler, objectives to the movement seems to be due largely to the Luddite novel *Ben o' Bills, A Luddite Tale*, published later in the century, where the movement's *raison d'être* is set out in terms perhaps more appropriate to the Declaration of Independence than to a conspiracy dedicated to smashing shearing frames:

'We are banded together . . . to asert the rights of labour, to resist the encroachments and the cruelty of capital. We seek to succour the needy and to solace the sorrowing. We aim to educate the toilers to a sense of their just rights, to amend the political, the social and the economic conditions of those whose only wealth is their labour, whose only birth-right is to toil. Our methods are persuasion, argument, united

---

[1] The 'reading of the Riot Act' was a formality usually felt to justify the subsequent use of force. It was carried out by a magistrate and required all those present to disperse.

representation of our claims, and, if need be, the removal of those mechanic rivals of human effort by which callous and heartless employers are bent on supplanting the labour of our hands. But this is only the last resort, all other means exhausted, our righteous claims, flouted, our fair demands denied.'

Aided, as already mentioned, by a good deal of sympathy, even among the literate, newspaper-reading classes, the movement had by the end of 1811 taken firm root around Nottingham.—'A mysterious organisation has been brought into existence', admitted the *Leeds Mercury* on the 21st December, 'which baffles every ordinary effort to suppress it. The rioters appear suddenly, in armed parties, under regular commanders: the chief of whom, be he whomsoever he may, is styled General Ludd, and his orders are as implicitly obeyed as if he had received his authority from the hands of a monarch'. By now the Luddites had added effrontery to violence. When a local committee promised a reward totalling £600 for information about the conspirators on top of £50 already offered by the Prince Regent, they retorted with a rival proclamation offering £2,300 'to anyone who would give them information of any person having given information to the Secret Committee'.

WHEREAS,

Several **EVIL-MINDED PERSONS** have assembled together in a riotous Manner, and **DESTROYED** a **NUMBER** of

FRAMES,

In different Parts of the Country:

THIS IS

TO GIVE NOTICE,

That any Person who will give Information of any .Person or Persons thus wickedly

BREAKING THE FRAMES,

Shall, upon CONVICTION, receive

50 GUINEAS

REWARD.

And any Person who was actively engaged in RIOTING, who will impeach his Accomplices, shall, upon CONVICTION, receive the same Reward, and every Effort made to procure his Pardon.

☞ Information to be given to Messrs. COLDHAM and ENFIELD.

Nottingham, March 26, 1811.

G. Stretton, Printer, Nottingham.

The second element in the rapid growth of Luddism was its secrecy. Recruitment to the Luddites, the subsequent trials revealed, usually began with men concerned at the threat to their livelihood agreeing to hold a meeting to discuss it, followed by private appeals—sometimes accompanied by threats—to others to join them, less to swell their numbers than to bind the tongues of potential informers. Here, as the evidence given in court makes clear, *Ben o' Bills* is a reliable guide, and the whole scene described below bears a close resemblance to that revealed in evidence at the trial of the Tolpuddle Martyrs twenty years later.

In *Ben o' Bills* the new recruit has been led past the guards at the foot of a staircase in a local inn to an upstairs room, escorted by his sponsor:

The long low chamber which we now entered was in darkness, save for the light of two small lanthorns, placed on a long narrow table that ran down the centre of the room. Forms ran round three sides of the room. At the head of the table was an armchair of ancient oak. In the centre of the table, flanked on either side by lanthorns, which turned their lights each to the other, was a human skull. In the chair sat one whom I felt rather than saw to be my cousin George. By his right hand was a Bible: on his left, one who acted as secretary. The forms around the wall were close packed by masked men, in working dress, who rose as Booth led me into the room and placed me at the foot of the table confronting the present. . . .

And this Number 20—it was the universal Luddite precaution on all occasions to identify each other only by number—duly does, in the terms already quoted—

'No 20, I call upon you to explain to this candidate the principles of our order.'
'Benjamin Bamforth', came my cousin's voice across the gloom. 'You have heard the statement of our aims. Are you willingly to ally yourself

with us and to aid us in our cause. If so, answer "I am".'
'I am. . . .'
'Place your hands, Brother Bamforth, upon the Bible and fix your eyes upon these emblems of mortality. As they are, so be you, if you falter, or if you fail. . . . Repeat after me the words of our oath.'

Then, phrase by phrase . . . I repeated . . . the solemn words:
'I, Benjamin Bamforth, of my own voluntary will, do declare and solemnly swear that I never will reveal to any person or persons under the canopy of heaven the names of the persons who comprise this secret committee, their proceedings, meetings, places of abode, dress features, complexion, or anything else that might lead to a discovery of the same, either by word, deed or sign under the penalty of being sent out of the world by the first brother who shall meet me, and my name and character blotted out of existence, and never to be remembered but with contempt and abhorrence. And further do swear, to use my best endeavours to punish by death any traitor or traitors, should any rise up among us, whereever I may find him or them, and though he should fly to the verge of nature I will pursue him with unceasing vengeance, so help me God and bless me, to keep this my oath inviolate'.
'Kiss the Book.'
I kissed the Bible.
'Show more light.'
'In each quarter of the room a light shone forth, its rays till now obscured.'
'Brethren, unmask, and let our brother know his brethren.'

New Year's Day 1812 was ushered in with rick-burning in Nottinghamshire, the traditional sign of rural discontent, and the attacks on machines continued. It was a brave citizen who challenged the culprits. When the wife of a man who had had seven stocking-frames broken 'swore to several persons as being concerned in the outrage . . . such was the indignation excited against her among some of the stocking-makers at Basford, that it was judged expedient to remove the family, with their furniture, escorted by the Military to Nottingham, as a place of refuge'. On the night of the 12th January 1812, when a group of fifty to sixty men were interrupted while smashing nine lace frames at Cartergate in the city itself, 'between seven and eight in the evening . . . on the constables coming up, one of the rioters presented a loaded blunderbuss and another a pistol and told them, if they attempted to interfere, they should receive the contents'. By the time reinforcements had arrived the Luddites had disappeared into the darkness, and 'were not more heard of until the following night at New Radford, where they demolished three frames, which were making a net contrary to their orders'. Similar incidents, over an increasingly wide area, were soon

an almost nightly occurrence until, by early March, a total of '42 lace frames' costing when new £60 each, and '544 plain silk and cotton frames', valued at £18 to £20 each, had been destroyed.

By this time industrial unrest had spread far beyond Nottinghamshire. In December the first systematic frame breaking had been reported from the adjoining counties of Derbyshire and Leicestershire. At Stockport, in Cheshire, a classic product, in its grime and rapidly spreading mean streets, of the Industrial Revolution, attempts were made to set alight to two factories and there were rumours of a general rising on the 1st May, already a red-letter day among would-be revolutionaries. No rising occurred, but one mill-owner's house was burned down and his steam-looms

Rick-burning in Kent, 1830

destroyed. In February and March, 1812, other factories were attacked at Eccles and Ashton-under-Lyne, Bolton and Huddersfield, Halifax and Horbury, near Wakefield, where 300 Luddites were seen 'marching in regular order, preceded by a mounted party with drawn swords and followed by a similar body of men as a rear guard'. At Sheffield, the Luddites equipped themselves with weapons by raiding the armoury of the local militia, and around Huddersfield and Leeds the rattle of musketry in the night as the Luddites held weapon-training sessions became a familiar sound. The characteristic Luddite weapon, however, was the hammer, especially the heavy sledgehammer used to batter down the doors of defended mills and to smash the machines inside, known as 'Enoch', after a famous Yorkshire blacksmith, Enoch Taylor, who had turned to machine-manufacturing. 'Enoch has made them and Enoch shall smash them'

ran the saying and one Luddite was reported (though the source seems semi-fictional) to have described this formidable tool as 'the best reasoner I know of'.

Recurrent rumours circulated at this time of men seen drilling on the Northern moors and this perhaps included training similar to that which other citizens, higher up the social scale, were receiving in the militia, for the machine-wrecking parties were soon displaying a mastery of simple tactics and of the use of cover which more orthodox armies might have envied.

'The Luddites', explained the *Leeds Mercury*, 'divide themselves into two parties, the more daring and expert of which enter the premises, provided with proper implements for the work of destruction, which they accomplish with astonishing secrecy and dispatch. The other party remain conveniently stationed at the outside of the building, to keep off all intruders, and to give the alarm'. The technique was

Enoch's hammer

displayed to advantage in one of their most famous attacks, made one Monday midnight in March 1812, on a mill at Rawden [i.e. Rawdon] seven miles from Leeds:

On entering the mill six or seven of the men, principally armed, seized the watchman and held him on the floor. The commander then ordered those who were not engaged in this service to 'Go to work' and they proceeded with all possible despatch to destroy the shears, of which they broke from thirty to forty pairs, and materially injured the machinery. Their purpose being effected, they assembled on an adjoining eminence and, after answering to their numbers dispersed instantly. This lawless proceeding was performed in about twenty minutes, in the course of which time, the depradators destroyed thirty six windows and injured three pieces of fine woollen cloth.

Two nights later came another attack, in Leeds itself, and this time the method was entirely different. 'The perpetrators . . . entered the premises', of Dickinson, Carr and Shann's finishing shops, 'from the roof, and, after effecting their purposes, lowered themselves out of an upper story by means of a piece of woollen', having 'torn and cut into shreds, eighteen pieces of fine cloth, dressed by machinery' worth 'from four to five hundred pounds'.

Despite increasingly generous rewards no information was forthcoming about those responsible and though formidable bodies of troops were soon billeted all over the affected areas they proved no match for the Luddites, with most of the population, whether from conviction or fear, on their side. An exploit typical of those which passed into local legend, and which discouraged any would-be informers from betraying them was described in the London *Examiner* in September 1812, apparently relating to

events near Nottingham some months earlier:

So sudden and alert were they in their movements, that a party of soldiers, who were frequently on all sides within call, did not know of their visits till the mischief was done. There was a curious instance of their dexterity in a village where a file of soldiers had been stationed and where two of those soldiers were watching a house, in which there were five or six frames. Four Luddites started on a sudden upon those soldiers, and while they pinioned their arms and kept their mouths shut, two others broke all the frames in a few seconds. They then retired with precipitation and the alarm was given by the soldiers; but in an instant, several of those soldiers, in pursuit, had their heels kicked from under them, and, after getting up, they heard the signal of the Luddites dispersing in a very opposite quarter. Having a perfect acquaintance with the country they completely eluded pursuit: and, in the instance of the great body of them crossing the Trent, and dividing their forces, the more effectively to accomplish their work of

£200. Reward

WHEREAS

The WAREHOUSE of Mr. William Radcliffe,
COTTON MANUFACTURER,
ADJOINING TO HIS DWELLING-HOUSE IN THE HIGHER HILLGATE,
STOCKPORT, IN THE COUNTY OF CHESTER,

Was, between the Hours of 2 and 3 in the Morning of FRIDAY the 20th of March, instant,

Wilfully, maliciously, & feloniously

Set on Fire,

By some wicked and desperate Incendiaries, who broke the Windows thereof, and threw in five Flambeaux or Torches, composed of Pitch, Tar, Oakum, and Spirits of Turpentine; and some Waste Cops of Cotton-weft, which had been dipped in similar Spirits.

The Villains left on the Outside of the said Warehouse, three Clubs or large Sticks of a peculiar Sort, which may be the future Means of a Discovery.

A Reward of £200. will be paid to the Person who may give such Information as may lead to the Discovery and Conviction of the Principals concerned in this diabolical Crime, upon Application to

J. LLOYD, Solicitor.

Stockport, March 21st, 1812.

LOMAX, PRINTER.

destruction, their route was detected, and soldiers were planted on all the probable crossing points of the river, to intercept them on their return. The outposts of the Luddites quickly discovered their danger, and communicated to the rest the trap laid for them; but they had provided for such a disappointment and had absolutely a milk boat hid in a winding corner of the river, by which they got over unperceived by a single soldier. The attacking parties had their faces either blackened or covered with crepe, but the outposts had nothing to distinguish them, or nothing about them by which they could be detected. I have never heard of one of them having ever been seized in their nocturnal expeditions and those who were detected were informed against afterwards, by some of those who had known them. One of these informers, by whom several were convicted, is said to have been very correct in his testimony; his life is in consequence, not in a state of the utmost safety; and he is obliged to skulk from one hiding place to another to prevent being discovered.

Adding to the Luddites' popularity was a much-publicised chivalrous streak; it was not for nothing that the favoured meeting place of the Nottinghamshire group was Robin Hood's former haunt, Sherwood Forest. 'There was', wrote the *Examiner,* 'one peculiar characteristic of the Nottingham Luddites that when they seized any provisions, ale or spirits on one night the party from whom they were taken was liberally paid for them the night following. There were a number of depradations, however, at the time, committed on the persons and property of people who were in no way connected with manufactures; but it is declared by the people of Nottingham, that those who perpetrated these crimes were not Luddites, but villains who took advantage of the confusion and alarm which prevailed, to attack houses merely for the sake of plunder'. The Luddites at this stage, in the eyes of their fellow workmen, could clearly do no wrong, though

many instances occurred later of men being forced to join them almost at pistol-point or being literally dragged from their firesides to take part in a raid, when they had had second thoughts after swearing the fatal oath. One man at least, who was later hanged, was forced to leave the bedside of his dying wife to join an arms-gathering posse.

Such excesses apart, however, the Luddites displayed throughout the movement's life, a remarkable loyalty towards each other; so-called 'informers' were often paid government spies who had joined the movement solely to betray it. Time after time, before the official espionage system became effective, suspects against whom the evidence was clearly overwhelming had to be released as no-one could be found to testify against them, and one trial, at the Spring Assizes in Nottingham in 1812, took place under outrageous intimidation. Late on a Saturday night, after the High Sheriff and his staff had unaccountably gone home, supporters of the men in the dock took possession of the courtroom, refused to allow any candles to be lit—presumably to prevent themselves being identified—and even pointed loaded pistols at the judge. He bravely declared that he could imagine no more glorious end than 'to die on the judgement seat in the execution of my duty', but lived to die in bed. The jury, less brave perhaps, acquitted the prisoners.

Occasionally a prisoner was rescued by force as in a famous incident near Stalybridge in Cheshire in May 1812:

On Tuesday se'nnight a person suspected to belong to this fraternity, was pursued by the peace officers near Staleybridge. Being a collier, he naturally retreated to his underground hiding-place, sliding for that purpose down the rope, hanging in the shaft of the pit. A guard of upwards of forty of the parole [i.e. police] were mounted at the mouth of the pit, which was kept up by necessary changes till the following Friday, determined to starve the besieged to a surrender, or confine him till death. On the night of Friday, however, a detachment of General Ludd's army, consisting of more than forty men, appeared, drove the besiegers from their post [and] gave a whistle, when the besieged ascended the rope and escaped.

Probably the most famous such escape of all was that of the incident remembered in Luddite annals as the case of the clock which struck thirteen. The escaper here was a young man brought before the magistrates on suspicion of having been concerned in a particularly serious attack on a mill. In court he produced a witness to prove that he could not have been involved, the sexton of a church who testified to his having seen him four miles away, at midnight, just after the attack, their meeting being fixed in his mind because the church-clock had at that moment struck thirteen. The local clockmaker confirmed that he had that day been called to service the defective mechanism and the suspected Luddite was released. What none except his close friends knew was that he was a champion runner and on that night, with the fear of death at his heels if captured, he had surpassed himself, covering four miles to the famous church—it was claimed—in nineteen minutes.

The spirit of fraternity among the Luddites was also manifested in their songs and one

Cropper's bench

Cropper's shears

which survives suggests that within their ranks they possessed men of literary, as well as military, aptitude:

Come cropper lads of high renown
who love to drink good ale that's brown
and strike each haughty tyrant down
With hatchet, pike and gun. . . .

What though the specials still advance,
And soldiers nightly round us prance;
The cropper lads still lead the dance,
With hatchet, pike and gun.

Great Enoch still shall lead the van,
Stop him who dare! Stop him who can!
Press forward every gallant man
With hatchet, pike and gun.

Chorus:
Oh, the cropper lads for me,
The gallant lads for me,
Who with lusty stroke,
The shear frames broke,
The cropper lads for me.

The 'cropper lads', living mainly in the Spen Valley in an area roughly within the triangle formed by Leeds, Halifax and Huddersfield, were the second group of workers among whom Luddism took root and they provided the movement both with its most striking successes and with what were to prove its final defeats.

'Cropping' might, in 1812, have been a trade made for Luddism. The croppers were skilled craftsmen who had acquired a virtual monopoly of the two processes involved in 'finishing' cloth, 'raising the nap', i.e. bringing up the coarser fibres of the wool, and then 'shearing' it, cutting it off with hand shears, 'clean and smooth to give a soft and almost velvety appearance and feel to the cloth'. It was a slow, time-consuming process, already out of date, but the croppers, or 'shearmen', had successfully resisted in many places ten years before attempts to introduce 'gig mills', which raised the nap mechanically, enabling the time needed to shear a piece of cloth to be cut from eighty-eight hours—well over a week's work for a man working alone—to twelve, little more than a day's work, though to achieve this he needed a boy to help him. Now the shearmen's second skill was in danger, for mechanical shearing-frames had been invented enabling a cropper, instead of using a heavy pair of hand shears weighing up to forty pounds, to do the whole job mechanically, using a moving frame, which 'travelled over the cloth', carrying several pairs of shears.

Looking back it is clear that this was the type of invention, vastly reducing the burden of labour, which in theory cloth-workers should have welcomed. But when, around 1811, a leading local manufacturer, William Cartwright, introduced cloth-finishing machinery at his water powered mill at Liversedge, near Brighouse, in Yorkshire, they became seriously alarmed. Week by week the work sent out to local workshops to be 'finished' dwindled and some establishments closed altogether, the employees being laid off. But resentment might have ebbed away into despair instead of erupting into violence had not a local journeyman cropper, William Hall, described as a 'very unmanageable young man' who had lost his job locally and found work in Huddersfield, brought back, on his Sunday visits to Liversedge, news of the fight the Huddersfield men were making against 'the cursed machines'. Under his influence the croppers assembled at their chosen resort, the *Shears Inn* at Hightown, to listen to Hall and to other, equally militant, workmates he had brought with him.

According to a later account—suspiciously verbatim, but probably not far from the truth—one speaker, an educated man, after

Cropping shop

recounting the Luddite victories at Huddersfield wound up with a practical suggestion:

'We have heard from our friends at Marsden that two more waggon loads of these frames are coming to Cartwright's place next week. . . . If you do not want the bread fliching from your mouth resolve now that that accursed load shall never cross Harshead Moor'. Those present thereupon took the Luddite oath, under the guidance of the Huddersfield men, who promised to ' "bring Enoch" ' along with other reinforcements 'and show them "how to go on" '.

Like the skilled commander he clearly was the Luddite leader from Huddersfield had ensured that the first attack by these new recruits should be a walk-over. The waggons were ambushed as planned, on lonely moorland as darkness was falling, and the drivers made no resistance and allowed themselves to be blindfolded while the hated frames were smashed into fragments.

Soon afterwards a similar meeting, attended by Luddites from all over the area, took place at another public house patronised by cloth workers, the *Saint Crispin* in Halifax, the principal speaker here being a man from Nottingham, who, it was said, denounced the aristocracy and claimed that Luddism was gaining ground all over Nottinghamshire, Lancashire, Derbyshire and Cheshire. He also asserted, probably with less justification, that its central council (of whose existence no proof has ever been found) was 'in daily

The Shears Inn, Hightown

communication with the societies in the centres of disaffection and they urge a general rising in May'.

According to the same report, one of the leading local Luddites then declared: 'We'll reckon with the aristocrats in London in due time, but . . . I know of no aristocrats who are bigger tyrants than our own masters, and I'm for squaring with them first'. He proposed as their immediate targets Cartwright's mill, which its owner had boasted of defending, and another leading local mill-owner, Thomas Horsfall, a sworn enemy of all Luddites, who had urged his neighbours to stand firm against their threats. Eventually a coin was tossed. It came down 'heads' for Cartwright; his mill, at Rawfolds, it was agreed, should be attacked first, the date being fixed at Saturday 11th April 1812, the time at 11 p.m.

Before the attack could be launched the Luddites needed more arms and the customary raids were organised all over the district, helping to alert the authorities, who had already billeted detachments of soldiers at inns close to threatened mills throughout the area, and, more important, causing the redoubtable William Cartwright to strengthen his defences still further. Before long Rawfolds Mill resembled an armed fortress rather than a textile manufactory. Outside it was partly protected on one side by a mill stream, kept nine feet deep by a dam, and large and solid gates, while the mill door was studded

Gig-mill

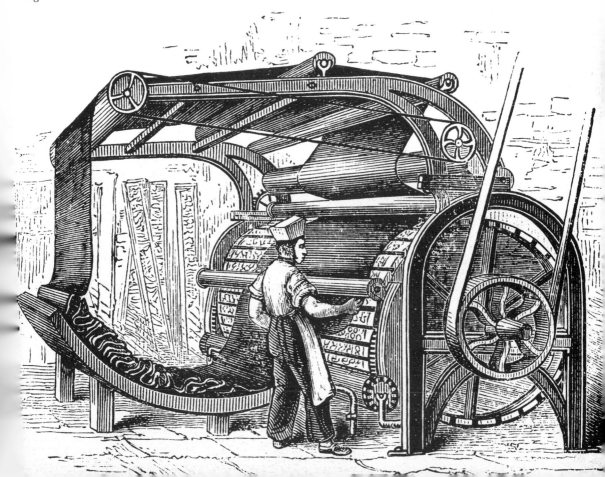

with heavy nails, guaranteed to tun the blade of the sharpest axe, and the ground-floor windows covered with barricades.

The real defences, however, were on the first floor. To prevent any attackers who broke in storming the staircase, 'rollers with spikes sixteen to eighteen inches in length' were fixed to it, while, 'huge carboys of vitriol stood at the head of the stairs ready to be poured upon the heads of any who should attempt to ascend'. Cartwright was clearly, like some of the leading figures on the Luddite side, a man who had missed his real vocation, the Army. A believer in defence in depth he had also fixed pulleys to the heavy flagstones of the floor so that they could easily be raised, to provide both a breastwork for the defenders up above and

holes through which fire could be poured down on the men trapped below. As a final precaution, a man was assigned to ring the mill bell to summon the assistance of the military, but, even without their help, Cartwright hoped to put up a stern fight in defence of his property.

The final Luddite preparations for the coming attack began at dinner-time on the appointed day when a messenger toured various workshops warning selected leaders that it was definitely 'on', and some men did not return to work, spending the afternoon in working out the details of the operation in an upstairs room at the *Shears Inn*. Throughout the preceding week arms had been collected and distributed and soon after 10 o'clock that night men carrying a

RAWFOLDS MILL.

variety of weapons, from heavy hammers to hedge stakes, as well as firearms, began to assemble at the appointed spot, a field near a stone obelisk at Cooper Bridge, known as the Dumb Steeple. By midnight, when they were due to move off, nearly a hundred men had been mustered, though another fifty had failed to arrive as expected. Detachments had, however, come in from most of the surrounding townships and villages, and a further contingent, from Leeds, was expected to join them later near the mill. In command was a man called George Mellor, one of the most radical and articular croppers, who had played a leading part in the meeting at the *St Crispins*. The Luddite historian, Frank Peel, (who was not present, but drew on the recollections of those who were) described the scene which followed:

The stragglers were called together by a low whistle, and Mellor's deep voice is heard as he puts them in order. They form in a long lane, down which the various leaders walk, calling over their rolls, not by names but by numbers. . . . They are next formed into company. The men with guns are called to march first, and Mellor assumes the command of this detachment. Next follows the pistol company. . . . A hatchet company comes after and the rear is brought up by the men wielding huge hammers, and by those who carry only bludgeons or are without weapons of any kind. They are rapidly put through a short drill and then formed into marching order, John Hirst of Liversedge, and Samuel Hartley, of Rawfolds, who was or had been in Cartwright's employ, being told off as guides. It is now approaching midnight and they have some three miles to walk so no time must be lost. Before giving the word to start George Mellor stands in front of the men and endeavours to fire their courage.

'We are all ready now men', he said in a deep, clear voice. 'You are all aware that we go tonight to wreak vengeance on the braggart Cartwright, of Rawfolds, who has so long taunted us and set us at defiance. . . . He has boasted again and again how he would defend his mill. . . . Nevertheless we are able to deal with him. . . . Now, lads, show us you know what to do!'

Instantly the first company placed their guns to their shoulders as if about to fire, the next company held out their pistols as if animated by a similar intention, and the rest uplifted significantly their great hammers and hatchets.

'Right men', cried Mellor, 'now march'.

They must, as they moved off, have made a strange sight for 'they were nearly all disguised, some having their faces simply blackened and others wearing masks to conceal their features. . . . Many of them were dressed in carters' smock frocks, others had their coats turned inside out, some had put their checked shirt over their clothes and a few had actually dressed themselves

The Dumb Steeple

partly in women's apparel'.

As the Luddites tramped through the dark lanes towards their objective, William Cartwright and his little garrison of four workmen and five soldiers had settled down to sleep there, in beds made up on the first floor, while two watchmen stood guard at the gates, and Cartwright's dog was posted in the room below. It was the dog which, just as his owner was about to fall asleep, gave the first alarm. Cartwright was at first inclined to disregard it, as he had heard nothing from the sentries on the gates, not knowing that the Luddites had sent forward guides, who knew the premises, to seize the two watchmen 'before they had the opportunity of giving any alarm whatever'. But Cartwright's faithful watchdog refused to be silenced and his 'low growling . . . speedily changing to furious barking', until his owner 'listening . . . more intently . . . could hear above the monotonous booming of the neighbouring waterfall a confused murmur. . . . Rousing his companions they at once prepared for the defence'.

Almost at the same moment, all attempt at secrecy was abandoned. George Mellor, after examining the heavy gates, 'gave the order, "Hatchet men, advance!" . . . and the stalwart band, bearing huge hatchets and great hammers on their shoulders, advanced to the front'.

A contemporary cartoon of the Luddites

'Now men', cried Mellor, 'clear the road.' Instantly at the word of command, the weapons, wielded as they are by powerful arms, come down upon the gates with terrific force. Soon the heavy woodwork flies in splinters and, anon, with fearful crash, like the felling of great trees, the first barricade drops prostrate and the rioters pour rapidly and steadily over it into the mill yard. A few paces and they look up at the great mill. Its long rows of windows glitter in the starlight, but all is dark inside and there are no signs of its defenders. It stands all black and still and nothing is heard but the furious barking of the dog, which has now changed to a frantic howl. . . . Then with a sudden and tremendous crash, hundreds of great stones come bounding through the long lines of windows and it seems as if every atom of glass and woodwork are swept away. Then follows a terrific yell from the desperate multitude. The echoes of that savage cry have not died away before the rioters fire a volley through the empty windows. The signal is now given to the defenders of the mill; the hitherto silent building wakes up and a steady peal of musketry echoes sharply through the valley. The rioters are half mad with rage; they have never been so set at defiance before.

They march in steady phalanx to the mill door. . . . Down come the great hammers once more with thundering noise, and the heavy boom almost drowns the sound of the alarm bell on the top of the mill. In their wild fury the hammermen strike not only the door but the stone door posts. The sparks fly at every blow, but there are no signs as yet of the staunch door yielding to their frantic efforts. Mellor and the other leaders are rushing about like wild men, encouraging the rioters who fire volley after volley through the yawning windows. Sheets of flame light up the interior of the mill at regular intervals and the frequent groans and cries which issue from the sheeting mass surrounding the walls testify to the accuracy of the aim. Mellor notes that the volleys come obliquely through the floor above, and that his enemies are safe behind their covers. They must try to take them in the rear.

'To the back, lads', he cries.

The defiant voice of Cartwright is heard in reply: .

'Come round, we'll meet you'.

And meet them they did. The back proved equally impregnable, and, with nine feet of water to one side of it, even more dangerous in the darkness than the bullets at the front. One man managed to climb up on a wrecked window, and got a musket ball through his hat as his reward, but this was as near as the Luddites came to storming the citadel and after a battle lasting half an hour Mellor, his ammunition almost exhausted, called off the attack. He left behind two badly wounded men, reminding them before leaving of their oath of secrecy, then the Luddites retreated into the darkness, desperate to get safe indoors before the military and the constables arrived.

Although, for the moment, all the remaining Luddites got clear away, news of their disastrous rebuff at Cartwright's mill spread, destroying both the myth of their invincibility and their own self-confidence. It was the Luddites' first defeat and in the long run proved decisive. The two men left behind at the mill both died within thirty-six hours, refusing, despite constant persuasion and, some whispered darkly, torture, to betray their comrades. ('Can you keep a secret?' one asked a particularly persistent clergyman, and on his interrogator leaning eagerly forward for the hoped-for confession, retorted 'So can I' and so died.) One of these victims was taken to Halifax for burial, and many of the town's working men turned out to escort his coffin, their arms draped in white, for mourning. The body of the other, at Huddersfield, was secretly hurried underground at six in the morning; the thousands who arrived for the ceremony at the advertised hour, noon, had to go away frustrated.

Frustration was to be the keynote of Luddite activities in the area from now on. A week later an attempt was made to murder the victorious Cartwright but both his would-be assassins missed, and the Luddites had to take what consolation they could from smashing thirteen pairs of his shears sent to Huddersfield for grinding. But it was an exploit claimed at the time as a success which was to have a fatal effect upon their fortunes in this part of Yorkshire. George Mellor, unfuriated by the humiliating failure at Rawfolds, longed to take revenge on the Luddites' other chief local opponent William Horsfall. Horsfall expressed such contempt for the Luddites that the children would 'run out in front of his horse and cry "I'm General Ludd! I'm General Ludd"', on which he would immediately fall into a violent passion and pursue the frightened urchins hotly with the horsewhip'. When a local manufacturer of cropping machines abandoned his trade after receiving 'a letter signed "Captain Blunderbuss" stating that "if he made any more such machines Ned Ludd would fire his premises and lay his works in ashes"'', Horsfall did not conceal his disgust, refusing the man's proferred hand with the scornful remark "I won't shake hands with a coward".

Even Mellor hesitated, after the fiasco at Rawfolds, to attack Horsfall's factory for it stood on a hill with 'cannon placed behind a wall, so as to command the entire frontage of the mill', but the man himself despising to take precautions for his safety, unlike

The Huddersfield Cloth Hall

his more timorous neighbours, could be attacked, and less than two weeks after the failure at Cartwright's Mill, Mellor, declaring that 'we are jeered and laughed at now' and must 'let some of them see that we are not a pack of scared old women' cajoled and bullied three workmates into joining him in ambushing the other mill-owner on his way home from Huddersfield. Hit by pistol shots in seven places, Horsfall lingered on for a day and a half, and then died. The effects of the murder were immediate. There was a redoubling of anti-Luddite precautions. Some mill-owners fastened sheet iron over their windows and, following Cartwright's example, installed a full time garrison and one even constructed a trap

The Luddites shooting Mr Horsfall

door over his water wheel, so that 'if the rioters had gained an entrance they would, on touching the flooring, have dropped through into the wheel race below'. More constables were enrolled to keep watch on suspected individuals and lights forbidden 'in any dwelling after nine o'clock in the evening' to make Luddite meetings and visits easier to detect. But far more important was the change in public attitude. Machine-breaking was one thing, assassination another. 'The cold blooded murder of Mr Horsfall', concluded the historian of the luddites 'appeared in fact to destroy all the public sympathy which existed for them at the beginning of the movement and everybody seemed anxious now to root out the society which had planned and executed the foul crime'. William Cartwright, who had first challenged the Luddites and lived to tell the tale, was already admired by his fellow manufacturers. He now became something of a popular hero, especially after two self-styled 'avengers' had fired on him on his way home from Huddersfield-though both missed. Later he became even more widely respected after he had intervened when a punishment of two hundred lashes was being administered to one of the soldiers assigned to defend his mill who had refused to fire 'because I might hit some of my brothers'. After only twenty-five lashes Cartwright had demanded that the bleeding and unconscious victim should be released, thereby saving his life. A public subscription was raised in the mill-owner's honour, producing the enormous sum of £3,000.

In spite of the falling off in public sympathy, however, machine-breaking and riots of various kinds continued throughout 1812, though many of the outbreaks blamed on the Luddites were probably no more than spontaneous protests against high prices, like that which the *Gentleman's Magazine* described at Sheffield in April 1812:

About forty or fifty poor men came marching in wooden clogs into the potato market where, their number being much increased, they began to throw potatoes in every direction, breaking the windows all round in the market-place and driving the farmers and others from the market. They broke open the potato cellars and emptied them of their contents. The soldiers took several of the ringleaders into custody and the Riot Act was read three times.

After this affray potatoes littered the streets and it was discovered that several cartloads had been stolen along with 'two or three sacks of corn and large quantities of butter and fish'. The most serious aspect of the affair—well revealing how what began as a protest against high prices could easily turn into something else—was an attack on the militia depot, in search of arms. None were found, but the crowd smashed such military equipment as they could lay their hands on and were only dispersed by the Hussars. The trouble spread next day to Barnsley, and was only put down by cavalry summoned from Wakefield and soon afterwards there was more trouble at Stockport. Food riots also occurred, a little later in the year, in the other great Luddite centre, the Midlands, and there was an interesting development, at Nottingham, in September, with the first appearance of women in the movement. Here 'the mob paraded the streets', the *Gentleman's Magazine* informed its readers, 'headed by two women, dignified by the titles of *Madam and Lady Ludd* . . . broke the windows of most of the bakers and flour sellers and compelled them to drop flour sixpence a stone.' The twin inspirations of such protests were well revealed that night, when 'the mob reassembled . . . and plundered Lord Chesterfield's game-keeper's house of some hams and firearms'.

Throughout the Spring and Summer of 1812, there was also a good deal of what might be called orthodox Luddite activity, but the Luddites were now ceasing to carry all before them. In an old-style attack on a mill, at Middleton near Manchester, the owner, modelling himself on Cartwright's example, not merely beat off the besiegers but shot four of them dead. Increasingly the Luddites hinted that they were preparing for some grand future operation instead of launching the modest, small-scale assaults in which they had excelled. Rumours continued about what happened on secluded moors late on Saturday night and in the small hours of Sunday, the favoured time for Luddite 'parades', and the disappearance of leaden pipes and roofs was attributed to the Luddites building up stocks for melting down into bullets. Raids for arms continued, but they seem to have become increasingly an end in themselves. Late in August 1812 the *Leeds Mercury,* which had in the past recorded so many successful Luddite exploits, carried what was almost an obituary on the movement: 'General Ludd (says our Huddersfield correspondent) it seems is either dead or in a very sickly state, for he never troubles us now.'

In February 1812 the government had taken its first positive steps against the Luddite movement with the introduction of a bill making frame-breaking a capital offence, a measure that easily passed into law despite an impassioned speech in the House of Lords by the poet Byron who declared that to enforce it would require 'twelve butchers for a jury and a Jefferies for a judge'. Other critics argued that it would make accomplices even more reluctant to betray the guilty and there was in fact

Four men against the Luddites
Viscount Sidmouth, Home Secretary

Earl Fitzwilliam, Lord Lieutenant of the West Riding
of Yorkshire

Sir Joseph Radcliffe, Bart. JP, the local magistrate
most active in hunting down the Yorkshire Luddites

William Cartwright, Esquire, the mill-owner who
inflicted the first serious defeat on the machine-breakers

little need for the new law. It was already a capital offence to attempt to demolish a building, though not merely to damage it—hence the importance of establishing, as at Cartwright's mill, that a Luddite gang had not merely smashed the windows but had pulled out the frames. The Luddites were also vulnerable under the laws in force since 1789 against illegal oaths, though only liable to transportation. The government had planned to make this, too, when combined with machine-breaking, a capital offence, but on the very day in May that the measure was to be debated the prime minister, the reactionary Spencer Perceval, was assassinated in the lobby of the House of Commons. Some Luddites openly rejoiced, lending fuel to the suspicion that the prime minister's murder was part of a Luddite plot and perhaps the signal for a general uprising, and, though they had in fact nothing to do with it, the crime led to a general tightening up of anti-Luddite measures. The anti-Luddite drive soon proved successful. Two men were hanged at Chester that month and eight at Lancaster, and two more transported. The real break-through, however, came in July with the arrival in Halifax of two government spies, posing as unemployed working men who, even though one gave his name, not very imaginatively, as John Smith, were readily accepted as Luddite sympathisers and enrolled into a local lodge. Soon afterwards the first of their new comrades were rounded up and, arrests followed throughout the Summer and Autumn. Then in October, came the authorities' greatest catch; George Mellor was detained, and charged with the murder of William Horsfall, his response being, it was said, 'Three cheers for General Ludd'. Soon several men suspected of complicity in the other most famous Luddite

Threatening letter to Mr Byrnny, foreman of a jury

outrage, at Cartwright's mill, were also in custody. Faced by this threat to the movement's existence, a good deal of Luddite energy at this stage seems to have been directed against recruits whose early enthusiasm, never perhaps very strong, had waned. Threats to kill men who failed to turn out when summoned became common and one unfortunate cropper, for example, who failed to parade for an arms-collecting expedition received a drawing of a skull and crossbone with the grim warning:
The roll has been called tonight and another black cross stands opposite thy name. Beware, or thy doom is certain.
This prediction soon proved only too accurate; the unfortunate recipient, dragooned into joining against his will, was later arrested and hanged. Others, however, acted first and anonymous letters began to reach the magistrates from men anxious to

On Spec^l Commission at York Castle — Jany 1813. —

3. George Mellor
Wm Thorp —
Thos Smith — } Convicted of Murder & executed. —

4. John Swallow
John Batley
Joseph Fisher
John Lumb. } Capitally convicted of Burglary — and recommended to Mercy by the Jury. —

5. James Haigh
Jonathan Dean
John Ogden
John Walker
Thomas Brook } Capitally convicted of beginning to demolish Wm Cartwright's Mill. —

Extract from records of York Castle

point the finger of suspicion elsewhere. Some of the men detained, either through fear or because they were no match for their interrogators, betrayed others, until by the end of 1812 sixty-six suspected Luddites were lodged in York Castle, with almost every town and village in the textile-manufacturing areas of the West Riding represented.

On 6th January 1813 the first of a series of trials of accused Luddites began. Outside in the snow stood row upon row of troops. Inside, in the crowded courtroom, illuminated at first by the thin wintry sunlight breaking through the windows, but later dark and gloomy, the Luddites were soon fighting for their lives.

By the standards of later generations, the trials were remarkably quick and the carrying out of the resulting sentences almost indecently so. The three men charged with Horsfall's murder were tried first, and though they advanced the classic—and hitherto almost always successful—Luddite defence of an alibi, the evidence of the fourth member of the murder gang was conclusive. Two days later, at nine o'clock of a chill January morning, with two troops of cavalry and supporting infantry drawn up around the gallows to discourage any last-minute attempt at rescue, the three prisoners were publicly hanged in a field behind the Castle. The occasion was all that the authorities could have hoped for. There was no demonstration of sympathy. Instead, most gratifyingly, the three prisoners publicly acknowledged their crimes. Even George Mellor, the arch-villain in the eyes of law-abiding citizens, revealed an unexpected nobility. 'Some of my enemies may be here', he told the silent crowd. 'If there be, I freely forgive them and all the world and I hope the world will forgive me'.

The succeeding trials, which began on the following day, proved equally satisfactory from the government's point of view. Of six men accused of administering an unlawful oath in the previous July (to, they now learned, an *agent provocateur*), only one, a lad of fifteen was acquitted, the five found guilty, who included a man aged sixty-six, being sentenced to seven years transportation. Three men accused of breaking into houses to steal arms, which in law might mean no more than terrorising the occupants into handing them over, were also convicted and sentenced to death. The evidence revealed the extent of the arms-gathering activities of the Luddites. One man, with a pistol concealed up his chimney and three pounds of gunpowder hidden elsewhere, had, he admitted, 'been regularly employed in stealing of arms for six weeks or a month'. The major trial, of eight men accused of having 'riotously assembled and begun to demolish a certain water mill, occupied by Mr Wm Cartwright', began on Saturday 9th January 1813, most of the evidence coming from an informer. All the accused denied being present and three were acquitted, after what seems to have been a perfectly fair trial. The remaining five, along with ten other men charged at the same time with similar offences, were sentenced to death. One was reprieved, the rest were hanged at York on Saturday the 17th January 1813. They met their end bravely, singing a hymn on their way to the scaffold and in several cases, publicly acknowledging their guilt. 'Friends, all take warning by my fate', said one, explaining that he had been led away by wicked men.

The briefest speech was also perhaps the most moving: 'Farewell, lads'. By two o'clock that Saturday afternoon it was all over, and the crowd, orderly but deeply moved, had begun to disperse.

Later the bodies were taken home for burial and as the carts carrying them back to the Huddersfield area rattled down the cobbled streets they were watched by silent and sorrowing crowds. Even at the subsequent funerals there was no disorder, and, these deaths proved the last. The authorities decided to show mercy to the seventeen men still in custody and, no doubt barely daring to believe in their good fortune, they found themselves released, with a warning that the indictments could be revived if they got into trouble again.

This was really the end of the Luddites. Although scattered attacks on individual factories still occurred, and there were even a number of would-be risings, all absurdly ineffectual, in the next few years, the mainstream of working-class effort was soon being directed into constitutional channels. The 'Battle of Peterloo', in 1819 was not fought over the introduction of machinery, but over a demand for the franchise.

It was the Luddites' destiny to march down one of the great dead-ends of history, the political equivalent of the search for the philosopher's stone. Perhaps the last word should be with William Cobbett, who in 1816, when they were no longer much more than a memory, addressed *A Letter to the Luddites*. 'In all acts of violence to which you have been led . . . you have greatly favoured the cause of corruption, which is never so much delighted as at the sight of troops acting against the people. . . . Machines are the produce of the mind of man and their existence distinguishes the civilised man from the savage'.

3 The Docker's tanner

The docker must have his tanner, and that long before January.

John Burns, Saturday, 7th September 1889

To those who do not depend upon it for their livelihood the sea has often seemed romantic. At closer quarters, however, it takes on a very different aspect, and to men who earn their daily bread, upon it, or beside it, it often appears a hard taskmaster, at once capricious and cruel. Of no group was this more true than the tens of thousands of casual labourers, close-packed in the 1880s in row upon row of mean streets in Poplar and East Ham, and Rotherhithe, around the London docks; their very survival seemed to be at the mercy of the vagaries not merely of the tides, but even, with sailing-ships still common, of the winds. A single day without work might leave him starving, so that the dock worker epitomised

South West India docks in the 1880's

in his way of life that struggle to survive which the Victorians believed to be the natural lot of man.

Although more comfortably-off citizens further West commonly referred simply to 'the docks', as a geographical entity, and 'the dockers', as a single category of workers, both terms were gross over-simplifications. London was at this time the greatest port in the world; in 1888 79,000 sea-going vessels had entered or left it, an average of 216 per day, bringing into, or carrying out of, the capital, goods worth £226 million. This vast trade was directed—a fact soon to prove of great significance—from close at hand, in the City of London, where the ship-owners, dock-owners and traders using their facilities, who were to some extent in competition and even conflict with each other, included several specialised groups with an identity of their own, like the tea-merchants.

Until 1888, the various dock-owners had competed for trade with each other, but they had then been united by Act of Parliament in a loose federation, designed

The London Docks in the 1880's

to manage the whole docks through a Joint Dock Committee. The Committee, with headquarters at Dock House in Leadenhall Street, in the very heart of the City, managed three groups of docks, the East and West India, the London and St. Katharine's, and the Victoria and Albert, the first two being on the North bank of the Thames, just to the East of the City, and the third being further down-river at Tilbury. Two other companies remained outside the Committee, responsible for the Millwall docks, in the Isle of Dogs, and the Surrey and Commercial Docks, on the far side of the river. There were thus three separate employing bodies managing seven separate docks, each with its own rules, traditions, and conditions of work, and to some extent, rates of pay, a complicated situation made even more bewildering by the existence of numerous sub-contractors, each with his little private empire.

The picture which the various groups of dock-worker presented to the outsider was even more confusing. The aristocrats of the docks, the watermen and lightermen who

Landing Australian frozen meat from Sydney

manned the barges on to which goods were discharged, had a high degree of security and earned excellent wages, of from £2 to £3 a week. A little lower, averaging around thirty-six shillings, came the stevedores, also in fairly steady employment, whose job, loading goods on shipboard, demanded skill and experience. Although not all of them belonged to a union, many did and there were two competing for their allegiance, the Amalgamated Society of Stevedores and the United Society for Stevedores, who often joined forces. Very different, and far less predictable, was employment on unloading ships, the job of the dock-labourer. These men were either employed direct by the dock companies, or taken on as needed by contractors called wharfingers, who received a fixed sum for unloading a particular cargo and thus had

every incentive to keep to the minimum the number of hands employed. Working relationships were also bedevilled by a network of traditional bonus payments, for handling particularly unpleasant or 'dirty' cargoes, or for completing unloading in less than the expected time, this latter, known as 'the plus', being a particularly fruitful source of disputes.

By no means all 'ordinary' dockers were badly paid. Charles Booth's *Labour and Life of the People*, first published in 1889, estimated that an average family needed 23s a week to enjoy a reasonable, minimum, standard of living. Dockers in fairly permanent work, on the books of one of the Dock Companies and employed direct might earn from 20s to 25s a week. Such comparative riches tended, however, to go to the 'preferred men', 'the ticket men', or 'the royals', who

A London slum in 1889

were on the books of one of the quay or warehouse foremen and were given priority whenever men were needed. The vast bulk of the labour employed at the docks was casual, so casual that no-one was even sure how many men regarded themselves as being primarily 'dockers', rather than members of another trade filling in between jobs. Charles Booth estimated that in Bethnal Green, around the three main docks alone, the casuals numbered 10,000, and the future Mrs Beatrice Webb, one of his investigators, found 700 'royals' at the West and East India Docks, against 1,655 casuals without 'tickets', and at the London and St Katharines Docks, 450 'preferred' men, compared to 3,250 others. On the Surrey side of the river conditions were different again, since the trade was largely in wool, timber and grain, for which rates of pay were higher, and the demand for men more regular. The docks as a whole, it was believed, provided a living of some kind for about 100,000 people, of whom a high proportion were ticket-less casuals, uncertain of any income from one day to the next.

To the riverside areas of the East End had gravitated all those who, having drifted to the capital in search of work, had found only hardship and poverty. Into single rooms, or perching like birds on the stairs of overcrowded houses, hence the nickname 'rookeries', were packed the shiftless, the permanently sick, the decent man down on his luck, the drunkard, the homeless, the hapless, the hopeless.

Later 'the docker's dinner' was to become famous—a herring of doubtful freshness— but many would have considered it a luxury.

A slum around 1900

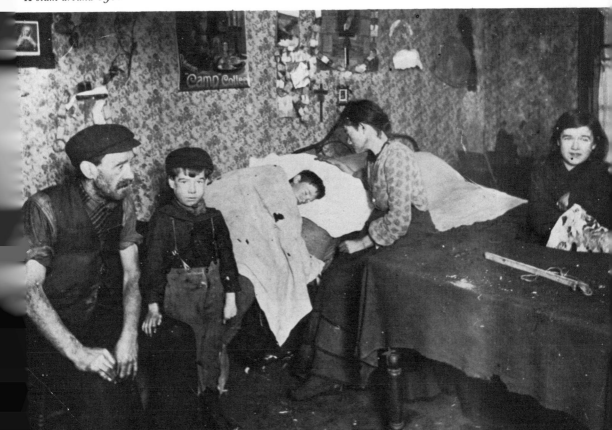

The staple diet of casual labourers and their families in dockland was bread, margarine, tea and sugar—the amount budgeted by a careful housewife for feeding her family was a penny a head per meal—supplemented, according to a dockers' leader, by 'refuse rice the coolies had thrown away'.

The lives of all this teeming underfed mass revolved round the 'call-on', the dock-gate cermeony held four times a day at which the foreman selected the men he needed for that shift. Everyone who witnessed it agreed that the call-on was degrading to all concerned. 'It was hateful to see that huge crowd of men collected at the dock gates from all parts of London', wrote one member of the employers' Joint Committee, while the General Manager of the Millwall Docks showed an equally compassionate attitude in evidence he gave to a House of Lords Committee in 1888:

The very costumes in which they present themselves to work prevent them doing the work. The poor fellows are miserably clad, scarcely a boot on their foot, in a most miserable state: and they cannot run, their boots would not permit them. . . . There are men who come . . . without having a bit of food in their stomachs perhaps since the previous day; they have worked for an hour and earned fivepence; their hunger will not allow them to continue; they take the fivepence in order that they may get food, perhaps the first . . . they have had for twenty-four hours. . . . These poor men have come on work without a farthing in their pockets; they have not anything to eat in the middle of the day; some of them will raise or have a penny, and buy a little fried fish, and by four o'clock their strength is utterly gone. They pay themselves off.

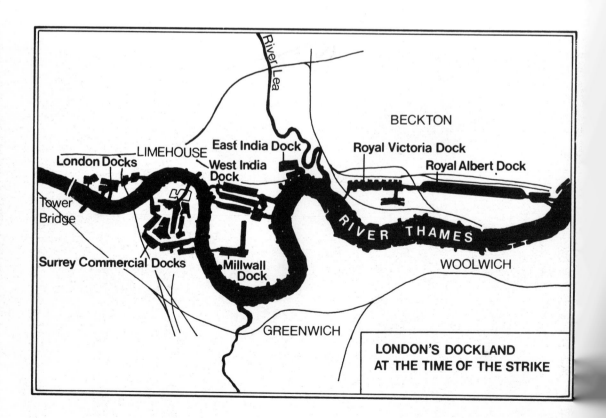

LONDON'S DOCKLAND AT THE TIME OF THE STRIKE

growing army of strikers marched around the riverside streets, led by improvised bands, bearing news of the strike to those still working at St Katharine's and the London Docks and at Millwall. As yet the Surrey side was unaffected, as was Tilbury, twenty miles down-river, and the press had barely reported what was happening. The real turning point came on the Friday. Ben Tillett had threatened, if his previous letters to the employers remained unanswered, to call for a reply with an army ten thousand strong at his back, and that morning, in the bright August sunshine, six thousand men formed up behind their bands and banners and marched in orderly procession down Commercial Road towards the City, pausing outside Dock House in Leadenhall Street to deliver six thousand hearty groans for the employers, followed by cheers for Ben Tillett as he led a deputation through the doors.

His reception inside was distinctly cooler. After a long wait he was told that the companies might consider the claim for a minimum 'call-on' of four hours sympathetically if the men went back to work, but there could be no question of a general rise in pay. The companies had lost the chance to contain the strike at the outset.

While Tillett was at Dock House, the procession was led on to Tower Hill by the most famous radical leader and popular orator in the country, John Burns, who has been well described as an 'agitator-of-all-work'. In 1889 he was thirty, a burly, black-bearded figure even more conspicuous than usual that day in a blue reefer suit

The secret of England's greatness—fivepence per hour! From the Bulletin *of 7 September 1889*

and a white straw hat, which became his trade mark. Like Thorne and Tillett, Burns was of humble origins, the son of a Lambeth washer-woman, though after becoming an apprentice riveter he had become a skilled foreman engineer (i.e. mechanic) employed on installation work abroad. At twenty he was arrested for holding an illegal political meeting on Clapham Common, at twenty eight, in November 1887, sent to prison after 'Bloody Sunday', when a man was killed during baton charges by the police trying to clear Trafalgar Square. In 1889, Burns, recently elected to the London County Council, was probably the most famous name in the whole labour movement. He was a man of aggressive self-confidence

and unshakeable conceit—he had a habit of pulling at the coat-tails of other speakers when he thought it was time he took their place. Later, in 1906, he proved a disastrous failure as the first working-man Cabinet minister, easily overawed by his colleagues and officials, but in 1889 he still possessed the charisma of a larger-than-life personality. An immensely hard-worker, as well as an inveterate self-publicist, Burns had regularly turned up at dawn at the dock gates to preach socialism to the dockers, but he believed they were incapable of organising to improve their condition themselves. When some time before, Burns had been asked to help in getting a dockers union started, his reply, according to Ben

John Burns speaking on Tower Hill

Tillett, was 'unprintable'. On Friday 16th August 1889, however, when news reached him that the impossible had happened and the dockers were out in force he did not hesitate. John Burns, with his eyes already fixed on Parliament—he got there three years later—was not the man to be left out at such a moment, and, hurrying down to Poplar, he joined Ben Tillett at the head of his procession to Dock House. By the time he had finished speaking on Tower Hill, standing on the seat of a stationary dray and waving his unmistakable hat, it was less Tillett's strike than Burns's. 'Stand shoulder to shoulder' he told his audience. 'Remember the match girls who won their strike and formed a union; take courage

from the gas workers who formed themselves into a society and only a few weeks ago won the eight hour day'. When a vote was called for on whether they should stay out every man's hand shot upwards.

Without outside support, however, any strike by the 'casual' dockers, was bound to be short-lived. They had no funds, no private savings, and as yet not even a union. The first essential, as Ben Tillett, who did most of the work, realised, was to persuade the two stevedores' unions, to call their members out, for this would not merely cripple the export trade but would demonstrate the solidarity of the whole labour force in the docks. Neither union had anything to gain from a strike; their members already earned

Dockworkers' procession

eightpence an hour and a shilling overtime. Both had much to lose: a long dispute would drain away their funds and an unsuccessful one might destroy them. But Tillett's persuasiveness and diplomacy successfully overcame their reluctance, assisted by the pleas of the two union secretaries, Tom McCarthy, of the United Society—Tillett's loyal ally from the first— and James Toomey, of the Amalgamated Society. All through Saturday the two unions' representatives deliberated in joint session, in an upstairs room of the *Blue Posts*, near the gates of the West India dock until, at midnight, James Toomey announced from a window, to a tumult of cheers and fireworks from the thousands of dockers massed outside, that the stevedores would fight alongside the dockers. Next day, Sunday, 18th August, the Executive Committees of the two unions formally ratified the decision and Ben Tillett, in an impassioned speech to a mass meeting outside the East India Dock, called for a mass walk-out by everyone working in the docks. Next morning the extent of the response became clear. The gangers, arriving for call-on, found not a 'casual' in sight. An unfamiliar silence hung over the waterfront for the first time in its history, and that day not a ship entered or cleared the port of London.

That Monday, 19th August 1889, the newly-appointed Joint Strike Committee began work in earnest. Its chairman, a tactful concession to the Stevedores, was James Toomey, and the members included the other stevedores' leader, Tom McCarthy, Ben Tillett, and a widely respected ex-labourer, Harry Orbell, who was sent to take charge at Tilbury. Also on the committee was the already legendary Tom Mann, another 'freelance agitator', a short but immensely powerful figure, widely regarded as the most dedicated and selfless of all the union leaders, who had learned about working class life the hard way. Born in Warwickshire in 1856, Tom Mann had been earning his living down the mines at ten, dragging on all fours a sledge laden with rubbish, but he escaped, to become a tool-maker and at twenty reached London, where he at first worked for a Brake Company, before becoming from 1885 onwards virtually a full-time, political organiser, paid by the Social Democratic Federation to travel wherever the gospel of unionism and political protest seemed likely to fall on receptive ears. Like Burns, his close friend and ally, he had no direct connection with the docks, but was called in to help because of his reputation as an orator and organiser—a reputation he rapidly confirmed. Also soon deeply involved in the strike, as co-opted members of the directing Committee, were John Burns himself and Herbert Hyde Champion, editor of *The Labour Elector*, a campaigning publication which had often carried evidence, collected by Tom Mann working as an undercover agent, of breaches of the law by employers. An ex-Army officer, Champion's thin and pale appearance and educated voice instantly marked him out from the tough-looking blunt-spoken working men who surrounded him, but he proved invaluable as the Committee's Publicity Officer, able to talk in their own language to the journalists who began that week to flock into the East End. For suddenly editors realised that what was happening in the Docks, almost on the doorstep of Fleet Street, was not a run-of-the-mill union dispute but a major social and industrial upheaval.

The role of the press was to prove vital in the struggle now beginning, but that

Monday morning publicity was probably the least pressing of the Strike Committee's concerns, as they talked and argued in the *Wade's Arms*, a sociable pub in Jeremiah Street, Poplar, where they had set up their headquarters. In the 'Bagatelle Room' a team of lady volunteers dealt with correspondence, and counted the coins from the collecting boxes, storing the coppers in a tea-chest. In the ground-floor parlour, H. H. Champion drafted his press releases, while in the kitchen soup or stew were perpetually simmering on the stove, ready, thanks to the warm-hearted licensee, Mrs. Hickey, one of the unsung heroines of the strike, to provide a hot meal for the members of the committee at any hour of the day or night. The two upstairs rooms, divided by folding doors, were the leaders' province, one being occupied by the Finance Committee in almost permanent session, the other by the main Strike Committee, meeting twice daily.

The Strike Committee's first reaction to what had happened must have been one of astonishment; the men had come out in a strength they had not dared to hope. But they knew that, like many earlier strikes, it could all too easily be broken by an influx of outside labour, scornfully dismissed by the strikers as 'blacklegs' or 'scabs' but not hard to recruit at a time when every street in East London, and every port in the country, contained unemployed men.

The most effective answer to blacklegs, as every union-man knew, was picketing and this became the special responsibility of Tom Mann. The dock companies, once they realised they had a major battle on their hands, had reacted swiftly. Posters appeared throughout the East End offering permanent work at £1 a week, an almost impossible dream of wealth and security to thousands of men at that time, while within a few days 'white-collar workers' in the docks were being mobilised to unload some of the held-up cargoes; the *Morning Post* reported that clerks from the counting houses, incongruously clad in frock coats and top hats, were busy unloading tea. A more serious threat was presented by men brought from other parts of the country, who might well feel that a dock strike in London was no concern of theirs. Intercepting these unwelcome visitors became a battle of wits between the dockers and the employers, for protecting every possible point of entry, especially the most vulnerable, like those at Tilbury, where the railway lines ran right into the docks, meant guarding a perimeter fifty miles long. Under Tom Mann's energetic direction the task was tackled like a military operation. A 'foreman picket' was made responsible for the defence of each dock and a regular picketing rota was prepared, only the most reliable men being entrusted with it and no-one serving more than twelve hours at a stretch. Tillett and his colleagues wisely decided to give preference in distributing strike pay (now beginning to come in as a result of public appeals and collections) to the pickets, who were paid from one to three shillings a day, and special task forces of pickets were organised to travel up and down the river to prevent blacklegs being brought in by water, and the local railways, alert for suspicious-looking 'foreigners'. Some even stood guard at the main line railway stations, to interpret men being brought in from other parts of the country. Only peaceful persuasion was permitted by law but it was interpreted somewhat widely. On at least one occasion, at Tilbury, one suspect train was stopped by four hundred men swarming across the tracks, until the twenty seven blacklegs aboard climbed out and surrendered. At East India Dock, two stevedores posed as blacklegs to reach forty men tempted to travel down from Liverpool by the promise of £6 a month, plus board and lodging, and persuaded them to go back; some in return for having their fare paid even agreed to picket the station there to prevent any more Liverpudlians making a similar 'mistake'. At least one cab bearing would-be strike breakers was diverted to the *Wade's Arms,* while others were dragged out of closed vans, or unmasked by having their hands inspected, when some 'City gents' in appropriate dress, proved to have remarkably gnarled and work-hardened palms.

Inevitably there was some intimidation. On Saturday 24th August *The Times* carried a notice sent to it the previous day by the proprietors of Hay's Wharf, where it had appeared:

NOTICE TO ALL MEN WORKING IN HOLDS AND ON THE QUAYS AS MEN,
We beg you to clear out at once, or we must inform you the consequences must be extremely serious.

If this were not intimidation, it certainly came very close to it. 'That a certain amount of violence *was* used, I am prepared to admit', wrote H. H. Champion in his contemporary history of the strike. 'You cannot pick some hundreds of men out of a crowd to perform delicate and responsible duties and be sure they will all temper their zeal with discretion. . . . The 'blackleg' in exercising his divine right to sell his labour for less than the rate at which other workers will consent to sell theirs, is inflicting upon them the most deadly injury one man can do another. . . . Even amongst the educated classes, there is very little love lost between competitors in business'. The dockers' critics made the most of such incidents as did occur and some alleged that only the threat of force kept the strike going at all. 'The managers of the London dock companies', declared 'A Wharf Owner' in *The Times* on 24th August, 'unanimously assert that the large majority of the labourers would willingly continue to work . . . were they not compelled to strike from fear of personal injury. Cannot a counter-agitation against the tyranny of such coercion be organised?' Another letter, appearing the same day from 'A Bonded Warehouse-Keeper' complained of 'the reign of terror' which prevails. . . . 'The tea and bonded warehouse keepers' labourers were ordered by a gigantic mob to turn out. . . . Our well-disposed workmen are now perforce earning nothing. . . . I hope that the . . . public . . . will withhold their charity to the strikers out of sympathy with those who would continue their work if allowed peaceably to do so. . . . Although during a long waterside career I have known several strikes', the writer summed up, 'I never remember one of the dangerous and revolutionary character of the present one'.

But 'the revolution' never materialised. Two thousand extra police were drafted into the East End, but they suffered nothing worse than having collecting boxes thrust towards them, and being publicly welcomed by John Burns, who predicted that they would enjoy a pleasant rest from their more arduous duties in the West End. The London Fire Brigade also took precautions:

its river floats were kept under full steam in anticipation that the strikers would fire the warehouses, but the only result was to waste a little coal.

The aristocratic, high-Tory, *Morning Post* comforted its readers on 22nd August with the assurance that 'in consequence of the grave apprehension felt by the dock authorities, the artillery and cavalry are under orders to be in readiness at a moment's notice', but the call to action never came. There is, on the contrary, universal agreement about the remarkably orderly behaviour of the strikers. The Home Secretary, an unpopular and obscure Conservative, Henry Matthews, refused to condemn as illegal the picketing in the docks and from 100,000 men directly or indirectly involved fewer than twenty were charged with breaches of the law and even fewer convicted. The Recorder of London, at the end of the strike, with not a single case arising from it awaiting his attention, paid the strikers a handsome tribute:

The whole history of the world does not afford so wonderful an instance of self-control on the part of suffering men with starving wives and children, and such discretion and forebearance on the part of the authorities. It is an instance of cheerful submission to the law which is a fit subject of national pride, and will forever do honour to all concerned.

Apart from picketing, the Strike Committee's main and continuing anxiety was money. An appeal for funds was made as soon as the strike began and a Finance Committee, including John Burns and Tom Mann, was elected on Tuesday 20th August. The first source of income was provided by the collecting boxes which were passed round at every procession or meeting, but, though the resulting jingling made an encouraging sound, most of the coins were coppers. The first collection, on Sunday 18th August, included a cheque for £1, but yielded no more than £6 2s 1d (£6.1), too little to provide even one penny relief per man. The start of press coverage in the following week brought the first sizeable donations rolling in, including £670 from John Burns's Amalgamated Society of Engineers, plus smaller sums, usually around £20–£30, from less well known unions like the East London Painters or the Friendly Society of Ironfounders. Later there were complaints that most British unions had come to the dockers' aid too late, when the strike's success was assured, but altogether £4,200 came from this source, easily eclipsing the modest £1,039 produced by street collections. The really remarkable feature of the strike, however, was the support of the general public, who had never before

SOUTH SIDE
CENTRAL STRIKE COMMITTEE,
SAYES COURT, DEPTFORD.
SEPTEMBER 10, 1889.

GENERAL MANIFESTO.

Owing to the fact that the demands of the Corn Porters, Deal Porters, Granary Men, General Steam Navigation Men, Permanent Men and General Labourers on the South Side have been misrepresented, the above Committee have decided to issue this Manifesto, stating the demands of the various sections now on Strike, and pledge themselves to support each section in obtaining their demands.

DEAL PORTERS of the Surrey Commercial Docks have already placed their demands before the Directors.

LUMPERS (Outside) demand the following Rates, viz: 1. 10d. per standard for Deals. 2. 11d. per stand for all Goods rating from 3 x 4 to 3½ x 7, or for rough boards. 3. 1s. per std. for plain boards. Working day from 7 a.m. to 5 p.m., and that no man take the "Red Lion" corner before 6.45 a.m. Overtime at the rate of 6d. per hour extra from 5 p.m. including meal times.

STEVEDORES (Inside) demand 8d. per hour from 7 a.m. to 5 p.m. 1s. per hour overtime. Overtime to commence from 5 p.m. to 7 a.m. Pay to commence from leaving "Red Lion" corner. Meal times to be paid for. Workways &c. Meal times double pay, and that the rules of the United Stevedores Protection League be acceded to in every particular.

OVERSIDE CORN PORTERS (S.C.D.) demand 15s.3d. per 100 qrs. for Oats. Heavy labour 17s.4d. per 100 qrs. manual, or with use of Steam 10s.1d. All overtime after 8 p.m. to be paid at the rate of ¼d. per qr. extra.

QUAY CORN PORTERS (S.C.D.) demand the return of Standard prices previous to March 1889, which had been in operation for 17 years.

TRIMMERS AND GENERAL LABOURERS demand 6d. per hour from 7 a.m. to 6 p.m. and 8d. per hour Overtime; Meal times as usual, and not to be taken on for less than 4 hours.

WEIGHERS & WAREHOUSEMEN demand to be reinstated in their former positions without distinction.

BERMONDSEY AND ROTHERHITHE WALL CORN PORTERS demand.

GENERAL STEAM NAVIGATION MEN demand:— 1. Wharf Men, 6d. per hour from 6 a.m. to 6 p.m. and 8d. per hour Overtime. 2. In the Stream, 7d. per hour ordinary time, 9d. per hour Overtime. 3. In the Dock, 8d. per hour ordinary time, 1s. per hour Overtime.

MAUDSLEY'S ENGINEER'S MEN. Those receiving 21s. per week now demand 24s., and those receiving 24s. per week demand 26s.

ASHBY'S, LTD, CEMENT WORKS demand 6d. per ten landing Coals and Chalk. General Labourers 10% rise of wages all round, this making up for a reduction made 3 years ago.

GENERAL LABOURERS, TELEGRAPH CONSTRUCTION demand 4s. per day from 8 a.m. to 5 p.m. time and a quarter for first 2 hours Overtime, and if later, time and a half for all Overtime. No work to be done in Meal Hours.

Signed on behalf of the Central Committee, Wade Arms.
BEN. TILLETT,
JOHN BURNS,
TOM MANN,
H. H. CHAMPION,
JAS. TOOMEY.

Signed on behalf of the South side Committee.
...BULLI...
...AS. H...
...UGH I...

side to be sent to Mr HUGH BRO.   Central Strike Committee, Sayes Court.

reacted in this way to a trade dispute but who from the very beginning took the dockers' side. Altogether nearly £10,700 flowed into the coffers at the *Wade's Arms* from private citizens, most of it direct, but some via collections organised by various newspapers, several of whom proved staunch champions of the strikers' case. Here, too, a newspaper appeal in support of a strike was a novelty, but the readers of the radical *Star* sent in no less than £6,700, and those of the *Pall Mall Gazette*, almost £700, with other donations from *Reynolds News* and the *Evening News and Post*. Among individual gifts were 2s od from 'Two poor bricklayers labourers', 12s od from 'a few Civil Servants', and £1 from 'Paddington Firewood Cutters'. Often people arrived at the *Star*

offices or the *Wade's Arms* to lay proudly upon the table a bag of coppers or a few shillings collected from their workmates. By far the largest source of funds, however, was that described in the official accounts as 'remittances from the colonies', which totalled no less than £30,423 15s od of the £46,423 15s od finally collected. The 'colony' which above all others provided the dockers with the means to hold out was Australia, where a wave of support for what one newspaper described as 'one hundred thousand men of our own race and a corresponding contingent of women and children . . . struggling for right' swept the country. Some mayors organised official funds, employers encouraged collections among their workpeople, and postmasters

Relief Committee isuing food tickets at the Wade's Arms

refused payment for cables to London promising funds. From Victoria alone nearly £20,000 was despatched to the *Wade's Arms*. The first of these vast, and largely unexpected, cheques began to reach London round about 9th September, just as the strikers' coffers were almost empty and spirits, after nearly a month of inactivity with no end to the strike in sight, were beginning to flag. From then onwards it was clear that at least the dockers would not be starved into surrender. When the strike ended there was still a comfortable £4,000 in the funds and, had more been needed, no doubt generosity in the dominions would have risen to the challenge.

At first, when the riches from abroad were still undreamed of, distributing the funds

Root's Coffee House

DISTRIBUTION OF FOOD TICKETS AT ROOT'S COFFEE HOUSE, HALF S⊺ POPLAR

THE GREAT STRIKE OF LONDON DOCKERS.
Sketched by our Special Artist.

received proved almost more difficult than collecting them. An attempt to provide relief in kind, namely bread and cheese, proved unpopular, but everyone was well aware that if cash were handed out a fair amount would rapidly vanish over the nearest bar counter. The solution was found in distributing food tickets, each value one shilling, which the local tradesmen agreed to accept as if they were cash, trusting the Strike Committee to redeem them. The first distribution of tickets was almost a disaster, for the hungry mob besieged Root's Coffee House from which they were being issued, desperate to get a ticket before the supply ran out. Order was only restored by Tom Mann. 'I put my back against one of the doorposts', he later explained, 'and stretched out my leg, with my foot on the opposite post . . . and passed each man in under my leg'.

Four thousand men received tickets that day, but soon the numbers looking to the Strike Committee for subsistence swelled far beyond this total, reaching 25,000, and eight separate centres had to be opened to serve them. Before receiving his ticket each man had first to join the newly-formed union, which was given the imposing official title of The Dock, Wharf, Riverside and General Labourers Union of Great Britain and Ireland. Its members, and the members of associated unions, like the Stevedores, formed, however, only the nucleus of the strike, for the prevailing excitement caused a whole series of walk-outs in other trades, many of them with no connection with the docks. The employees of Lloyds tinplate mills in Bermondsey came out; so did some printers' labourers, followed by the employees at a jam factory, and the makers of Spratt's Dog Biscuits, who swarmed along the streets bearing a toy dog with a

biscuit hanging from his neck. The coal porters not merely in the docks but in the main coal distribution depot at Kings Cross and St Pancras stopped work, causing the General Manager of the Gas Light and Coke Company to warn in *The Times* of 'the inconvenience and positive danger which will result to the entire metropolis if . . . our coal supply is stopped and London be . . . put in darkness'. Even when coal did arrive, however, the gas supply remained in jeopardy for the newly unionised gas workers were contemplating coming out in sympathy.

By 24th August it was, said *The Times*, 'reported that between 40,000 and 50,000 men are on strike', and on 28th August John Burns claimed that 150,000 men were out, though this total must have included many non-dockers. Only a fraction of these were fed by the Strike Committee, or by the voluntary organisations and private individuals which now opened soup kitchens in the East End or provided free breakfasts for several hundred women and children at a time. The rest like the stevedores, who refused to touch the main strike funds, must have lived on savings, or by pawning their few possessions. An index of prosperity in East London had always been the number of children wearing boots and now not merely were barefoot infants seen on every side but many homes were completely bare, with their whole contents in the pawnshop. One pawnbroker, unexpectedly displaying the union spirit, promised to

Spitalfields soup kitchen

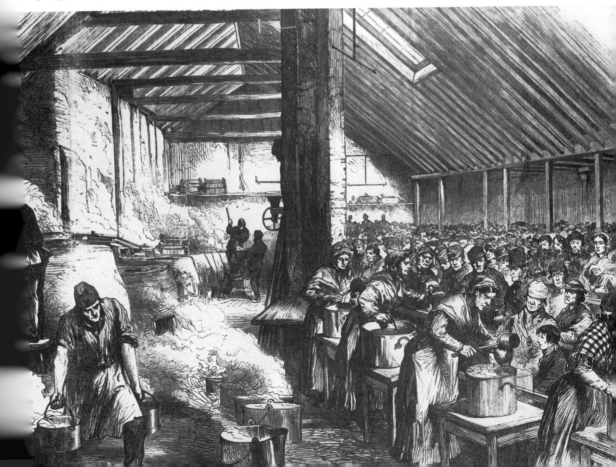

charge no interest until the strike was over.

The dockers' leaders soon worked out an effective daily routine for managing their vast army and keeping it out of mischief. The leaders themselves were up early, at five or six, 'making the rounds of the docks, visiting the pickets, addressing the men who were about, and recovering their voices lost overnight', according to the strike's principal historians, two Civil Servants who observed it at close quarters. 'After breakfast, . . . which was usually the only square meal of the day', they made their way to Tower Hill, 'the Trafalgar Square of East London', where the men had already assembled.

An ample road-way . . . dips down the western side of the square in the direction of the river. Alongside of it, with a background of sombre tea warehouses, runs a level road, surmounted by a broad stone parapet. At ten o'clock Tillett and Burns appeared on this upper road, which formed a kind of platform, but before they could gain the vantage ground of the parapet they were surrounded with a cluster of people who had

assembled to waylay them; dock labourers with grievances or difficulties, wharfingers with suggestions for a compromise, merchants or shipowners in desperation about their cargoes, individuals with a solution of their problems, philanthropists . . . who must put their gifts into Burns' own hands, and journalists yearning for 'copy'. . . . A word to one, a nod to another, a promise to a third, a little hand-shaking, and the levee being good-naturedly hustled aside, the parapet was mounted, the crowd closed up behind and the men, four or five thousand strong, who blocked the road below, put out their pipes, gave a cheer, and settled themselves for business.

After 'the news up to date in short, sharp picturesque sentences . . . and the weather forecast' the men received their orders in simple 'military terms', well-suited to a crowd in which 'many . . . had served with the colours or before the mast. . . . "Now you lads", said Burns, on one of the blackest days of the fight . . . "there have been complaints of the procession taking up too much room. Now there's to be no walking on the pavement, and only five deep in the procession. The roads are rough, and your

Sweethearts and wives waiting in support of the strikers

Dockers' children

DOCKERS' CHILDREN WAITING FOR BREAKFAST
IN WEST INDIA DOCK ROAD
Sketched by our Special Artist.

Dock labourers on strike, 1889

boots aren't much to boast of, I know, but five deep you must march, and no more. Now you stand still for a minute. If a man of you budges I'll stop his relief". The men grinned and stood stock still'. The oratory was equally direct. ' "What more do we want?" asked Tillett, in a fine vein of Jingoism, "we've got the ships, we've got the men, and we've got the money too".'

Then came the main business of the day, the return to the East End along a route carefully planned, to obtain the maximum audience for the strikers, and enlivened by 'floats' and fancy-dress to attract attention and turn what could have been a chore into a carnival. It served other purposes, too, as the strike's historians realised:

The strike procession . . . kept masses of men occupied and interested, a matter only second in importance to keeping them fed, and it was a grand opportunity for enforcing a respect for order and discipline amongst the heterogeneous dock populace, who had never known before what it was to fall into line, to follow their leaders, or, indeed to have any leaders to follow. The procession was timed to arrive in the city at about one o'clock. Passing up the Commercial Road at a swinging pace, which made the Metropolitan Police glad to give over their charges to the brethren of the City force, the pace was slackened gradually as the thoroughfare narrowed. At the entrance to Leadenhall Street the men had to trudge close to one another's heels. Penned in the trough of stately offices the music of the bands became more boisterous. No wonder such of the City as was left in town went to its lunch with some misgiving. It was disquieting to have the 'degraded dockers' marching past your office in tens of thousands, with the miscreants of Trafalgar Square leading them, while the windows rattled with the *Marseillaise*. . . . But the City soon learnt to take its invasion with equanimity, and, as soon as the strains of the band were heard, steps and pavements became black with every description of city man, from the magnate to the office boy.

The initial fear and hostility were soon replaced by tolerance and even sympathy. The 'docker's dinner', a rotting herring on a pole, told its own story, as did the obvious poverty of many of the marchers, but even more effective in winning over respectable opinion was the peaceful conduct of the marching thousands. H. H. Champion, the strike's public relations officer, observed its effects for himself:

Though there was little public sympathy shown in the earlier days of the strike, as soon as it became widely known that thousands of the strikers had marched through the City without a pocket being picked or a window being broken . . . the British citizen felt he might go back to his suburban villa when his days work was done with the full confidence that his warehouses would not be wrecked in the night, and that he could afford to follow his natural inclination and back the poor devils who were fighting with pluck, good humour, and order against overwhelming odds. One day in the City I was watching the long procession as it passed the Dock House in Leadenhall Street. With me was a City man of great respectability and strong Conservative views. . . . This man was losing a great deal of money and suffering enormous inconvenience every day the strike lasted. When he saw the men cheering, instead of hooting, as they passed the Dock Committee's headquarters, 'By Jove', he said, 'you know this is better than the barricades'.

The procession, here described by the strike's main chroniclers, soon became one of the sights of London:

First came a posse of police behind whom the marshals of the procession, with axes and scarves, reserved a clear place for the leaders. . . . Next came the brass band of the stevedores, following which streamed the multitude whose calling lay at the docks and riverside. Such finery as they boasted in the way of flags and banners had been lent by friendly and trade societies and this gave the procession the appearance of a great church parade or demonstration of The Ancient Order of Foresters. There were burly stevedores, lightermen, ships painters, sailors and firemen, riggers, scrapers, engineers, shipwrights, permanent men got up respectably, 'preferables' cleaned up to look like 'permanents', and unmistakable 'casuals' with vari-coloured patches on their faded greenish garments. . . . Doggett's [Thames race] prize winners, a stalwart battalion of watermen marching proudly in long scarlet coats, pink stockings and velvet caps, with huge pewter badges on their breasts, like decorated amphibious huntsmen; coalies in waggons fishing aggressively for coppers with bags tied to the end of poles; a brother coalie in effigy attached as figure-head to one of their vehicles, placarded with the announcement that he wouldn't go a step higher up the ladder . . . till the dockers had got his tanner; skiffs, mounted on wheels, manned by solid watermen; ballast heavers laboriously winding and tipping an empty basket, Father Neptune on his car in tinsel crown and flowing locks, surrounded by his suite—Britannia in a Union Jack skirt, the doctor in a faultless hat . . . and the barber brandishing a huge razor. . . . Emblems quaint and pathetic were carried in the ranks, the docker's cat and the sweater's cat, the docker's dinner and the sweater's dinner, the docker's baby and the sweater's baby, diminutive and ample respectively; Sir Hardwood (a gentleman understood to be connected with the Joint Committee) attired in mortar board, gown and mask, gravely saluted the bystanders and bowed low in front of the Dock House. The bass dressers, locked out for forming a union, brought up the rear, carrying their bass brooms like lictors. Such was the strike procession.

Although aware that they had lost the battle of public opinion, with even those who would normally have supported them showing sympathy with the strikers, the dock-owners were slow to offer terms, largely because some of them genuinely believed that a general rise in pay would so increase charges that traffic would be driven away from the port. Even that staunch member of the Strike Committee, H. H. Champion, sympathised with them in their dilemma:

I cannot help thinking that the dock directors have been treated more hardly than even they deserved. . . . They might well think that if they were to be required to pay . . . a rate arbitrarily and suddenly demanded by the men (and judged to be fair by the large proportion of the community *who held no dock shares*) that the end of all things was come. If they were to be execrated for paying 5d an hour and not giving regular employment, while they were making very small dividends on their capital, what was to be said of railway companies that work fog-signalmen twenty-two hours at a stretch at $2\frac{1}{2}$ an hour, while they enjoy a safe six per cent? To chemical manufacturers, who make 50 per cent on their capital, while paying less than 5d an hour for arduous and unhealthy toil? To match manufacturers, whose $17\frac{1}{2}$ per cent is earned for them by women, working for a penny an hour? Or to the entire female population, whose delight it is to spend hours in searching where they may buy articles of clothing at prices that are entirely incompatible with a living rate of wages for the workers who produce them?

But, whether or not it was the dock employers' misfortune, rather than their fault, to be made the scapegoats for generations of exploitation of unorganised workers, the strike went on, favoured by chance, as well as good planning. 'We were', admitted Champion, 'extraordinarily fortunate in the matter of the weather. It is not often that we get five weeks of uninterrupted dry and fine weather in Autumn in London . . . and this made an enormous amount of difference in the spirits and good temper of the men, while it deprived the dock companies of an ally almost as powerful as hunger, i.e. cold. A bitter east wind, or a drenching downpour, will take the courage out of a crowd in a way that the most fervid oratory can do little to counteract'. The strikers were also helped by a factor they *had* foreseen. The docks that August were exceptionally busy, so the companies needed all the men they could get and were conscious with every day that passed of business being lost.

At first the employers had been confident that the men would return within a few days. 'When the pinch comes, as come it must on Saturday', their spokesman told the *Morning Post* that first week, looking to the hungry weekend ahead for many dockers, '. . . I shall be surprised if there is any backbone left in the agitation'. A week later, one of his fellow directors was equally confident. Asked by a *Pall Mall Gazette* reporter 'How long can you hold out against them?' he replied cheerfully 'Why, a thousand years'. It was, he said, 'essentially unjust and unreasonable for the men to demand at this crisis a larger share of non-existent profits'. But if the profits *were* non-existent—and the dockers were always sceptical about such claims—the fault, many users of the docks believed, did not lie with the men. In the high-Conservative *Standard* on 26th August one merchant, acknowledging that 'the labourers have a cause of complaint', suggested that if the dock-companies would be hard hit as they feared by granting the men's demands 'the merchants . . . I think, would come to their assistance by relinquishing half the importers' discounts'. Another correspondent also urged a settlement: 'The poor men's demands appear to be most reasonable. . . . It is not the poor men's wages that absorb the profits, but . . . the excessive capital invested in the docks, bad management, excessive salaries to the higher officials, etc.'. The equally Conservative *Morning Post* reported on 22nd August that many shipowners were in sympathy with the strikers, and on the 27th a speaker at a meeting of one of the leading shipping lanes declared that 'We cannot but feel that there is an admitted grievance which ought to be put right. . . .

The proper people to do this are the dock companies, but if they cannot manage their own labour, why should not the shipowners do it?'

The first sign of an end to the strike came late in August, when one particularly enterprising wharfinger, well known as a good employer, Henry Lafone, organised a meeting between some of his fellow wharfingers and representatives of the Strike Committee which gave the men all, and more, than they had originally asked: two shillings per call-on, for a minimum four-hours, thus conceding the famous 'tanner', and a minimum guaranteed wage for 'permanent' men on the register of 24 shillings a week. It seemed as if the strike might be over, but, under pressure from the dock companies, all but ten of the 86 wharfingers repudiated the agreement.

The Strike Committee were doubtful at first whether to allow men to return to work even in the few wharves which had accepted the new terms, since this meant breaking the solidarity of the strike, but finally announced that work could restart at any wharf or dock accepting the Lafone Agreement, provided the men concerned gave the extra penny an hour they would now be earning to the Strike Fund.

While Lafone was still negotiating for the wharfingers the Dock Companies also made their first offer of terms, on Thursday 29th August. Men taken on before noon, they proposed, should earn a minimum of 2s 0d, for four hours' work or less, and 'as far and as soon as practical', 'contract work', paid at 5d per hour—the work normally done by casuals working for outside contractors—would be converted into piece-work, paid for at the rates the men were asking, at 6d per hour, and 8d overtime, which would apply between 8 p.m. and

8 a.m. Although the terms went some way towards meeting their demands, the Strike Committee unhesitatingly turned them down. 'The men', said John Burns, 'have demanded an irreducible minimum and are more hopeful and determined than ever'— the 'irreducible minimum' including an immediate payment of 6d per hour for all dock work, and overtime rates from 6 p.m. to 6 a.m.

Behind the scenes, however, the Strike Committee must have been tempted to compromise. On relief alone they were now spending at the rate of £1,250 a day, far beyond what was coming in. 'Hunger was playing havoc', wrote the strike's historians. 'The grief and despair in many a docker's heart contrasted grimly with the gay banners and lively tunes of the processions'. The notice posted outside the Committee's headquarters told its own story: No further relief would be given that day.

Lights burned late at the *Wade's Arms* that night. The Strike Committee feared that the public would consider the men were holding out unreasonably and, while they met, news reached them that the labourers at Wapping were threatening to go back. Ben Tillett hurried off to crush the revolt, and, in his absence, the Committee, conscious that funds were running short, decided on a desperate throw: an appeal to the whole working population of London, to go on strike unless the employers granted the men's full demands within twenty-four hours. It was after

London docks at night

midnight before Champion went downstairs to draft what became known as the 'No Work Manifesto', which was then signed by Burns, Mann, and 42 other leaders of the strike, and 2 a.m. on the morning of Friday, 30th August, before Tom Mann reached Ben Tillett's house at Bethnal Green and got him out of bed to add his signature. According to Tillett he was 'dead-beat and having only just been rudely awakened . . . did not then grasp the full importance of the Manifesto'.

Mann then went on to rouse a printer, who ran off copies at once and as those not on strike in East London made their way to work next morning they saw the document already plastered on the walls. The reporters now thronging the East End saw it, too, and the results nearly proved disastrous to the dockers' cause. Walk-outs in support of the dockers were one thing, a General Strike threatening the whole working and daily life of London quite another. Perhaps, many sober citizens began to feel, those who had warned that the whole outbreak was really a revolution masquerading as an industrial grievance, were right after all. 'Mr Burns', warned the *Morning Post,* 'is a kind of pinchbeck Danton threatening London with another reign of terror'. The agitation for improved conditions for the dockers had become a 'sinister and formidable movement'. Even more serious from the Strike Committee's point of view was the reaction of other unions, particularly the old-established, more conservative ones, which had long viewed with distrust the activities of new-style agitators like Burns, who were politicians first and trade unionists second. The Liberal *Daily News* reported that the senior officials of other leading unions 'declared the Manifesto to be a mistake', and insisted 'We are not all

Socialists'. Many unions protested privately to the Strike Committee that they should have been consulted before any such appeal were issued. Every responsible trade unionist knew that encouraging local militants to act in defiance of their officials was a recipe for chaos, that could threaten the very existence of a union.

At a dock-gate meeting that Friday afternoon John Burns blustered that he took full responsibility for the Manifesto and the crowd eagerly shouted their support for it— but behind the scenes Ben Tillett at least was wondering how it could be disowned. And then, unexpectedly, the chance came. The first £250 arrived from Australia with telegrams promising more to come. The strike it was clear, could be kept going a long time yet, and, with the overseas support as an excuse, the No Work Manifesto could be withdrawn.

But the damage had been done. The Dock Companies, which hitherto had adopted a distinctly superior attitude towards the press, suddenly began to court it. A room was assigned to reporters at Dock House, twice-daily statements were promised from now on, and a tour was arranged of those docks where, thanks to blacklegs or 'white-collar' help, some work was still going on. The wharfingers and others who had been wavering before accepting the Lafone terms to end the strike now announced that they would stand firm behind the Joint Committee. And on Friday 30th August, Burns and Mann, accustomed to being treated as the emissaries of a formidable, if not a victorious, army, were kept hanging about in a waiting room until curtly told that there was no question of a settlement on their terms and that henceforward the employers would talk only to 'any of their servants . . . selected by the general body', i.e. to the dockers' own delegates, not outsiders like Burns.

The strike went on, in an atmosphere of growing bitterness. In a rally in Hyde Park that Sunday, 1st September, in which he announced the withdrawal of the No Work Manifesto, Burns described the employers' spokesman, C. M. Norwood, as 'that rat' and declared that 'the strike would never be finished until Norwood and all his crew had climbed down. . . . Chastened by poverty', he promised, 'disciplined by suffering, the strikers will march on'. He then descended from the platform to take the collection himself in his famous straw hat, before leaving, amid loud cheers, in a carriage.

The carriage had been sent by the head of the Roman Catholic hierarchy in England Cardinal Manning; just at the moment when the two sides in the great struggle seemed irreconcilable the ideal conciliator had emerged.

Henry Edward Manning was at this time a man of eighty, a frail but still dignified figure, respected even outside his own church, and idolised as a near-saint within it. Unlike many eminent ecclesiastics he had a reputation as a campaigner against social injustice on the part of the rich as well as against such mainly working-class sins as drunkenness. Ben Tillett had claimed on 30th August, as proof that the men were not revolutionaries, that 'Cardinal Manning has been throughout a most cordial sympathiser with us'. Manning had in fact called on the dock directors earlier that day to plead for an end of the strike. But they were riding high after the blunder of the 'No Work Manifesto' by their opponents and it had not been a successful visit, as one of those present, who personally sympathised with the strikers, was forced to admit:
He made a very eloquent speech, but struck a completely wrong note. He knew nothing of the rights and wrongs of the dispute. He treated us Dock Directors as if we were a merciless money grabbing set of men, only caring for the profits of the company and not caring how much we ground down the men, and . . . he failed to make any impression. It would have been better if he had never intervened.

Manning himself was aware that his efforts had been a failure. 'Never in my life', he admitted, 'have I preached to so impenitent a congregation'. But he persevered and on Friday 6th September joined the Conciliation Committee just set up by the Lord Mayor of London, the traditional arbitrator in disputes that threatened the business life of the City of London. Besides the Lord Mayor and the Cardinal, the Committee included the Deputy Lord Mayor, the Liberal M.P. for Poplar, Sydney Buxton, the Bishop of London, Dr Temple (father of the future Socialist Archbishop William Temple, but himself distinctly to the right), and Sir John Lubbock, President of the London Chamber of Commerce. Perhaps under the influence of Manning, it realised from the first that, since the dockers could not, without disastrous loss of face and indeed virtual surrender, compromise over the amount of their claim, the only area for negotiation lay in the date of its introduction. At a meeting at the Mansion House Burns and Tillett were induced to accept that the famous 'tanner' might, perhaps, not be conceded at once, though they firmly rejected the first date suggested, of March 1890. With Manning being by turns, according to Tillett, 'patient, persuasive, but very very fair', both to the 'harsh and unsympathetic' Bishop Temple and the 'thrusting aggressiveness of Burns' the gap was gradually narrowed, and a possible compromise date, emerged, 1st January. Burns and Tillett left, to put this to the

Strike Committee, while Manning and his colleagues promised to consult the dock companies.

The result next day, on Saturday 7th September, was not encouraging. Without waiting to hear from his colleagues Burns told a reporter that morning that 'the docker must have his tanner and that long before January', while later that day the other strike leaders proved distinctly cool towards the proposal. The dock directors, meanwhile, although reluctantly, had decided to accept it. They would, they announced at five o'clock, sign a new agreement dating from the New Year provided the Strike Committee agreed to do the same, but the offer would be withdrawn if not accepted by midnight.

This was enough in itself to make it unacceptable. The Strike Committee could not possibly consult all the unions involved in the time allowed. Instead, however, of courteously explaining the situation to the Conciliation Committee, Burns and the other strike leaders, alarmed by the spreading rumour that the strike was over and the danger of a widespread return to work, decided to issue another Manifesto, which described as 'absolutely untrue' reports that a settlement had been reached and referred somewhat contemptuously to the Conciliation Committee. This abrupt and public repudiation of their efforts caused great offence to its members, who concluded that Burns and Tillett either had no real power to negotiate or were willing to go back on their word whenever it suited them. The Committee issued that weekend an indignant letter to the press:

Conciliation Committee

We are at a loss to understand how Mr. Burns and Mr. Tillett can have appended their names to a manifesto which is a repudiation of what we all understood they had agreed to, and should they persist in continuing the strike we feel they will have justly have forfeited the sympathy which has hitherto been shown to them and to their cause.

For the second time a gulf seemed to be opening between the strikers and the general public. Few ordinary citizens turned out that Sunday to hear Burns address a large rally of strikers in Hyde Park, though the men, stirred, as usual, by his eloquence, remained loyal and, at his suggestion, unanimously carried a resolution not to return unless promised the 'tanner' from 1st October. Next morning, Monday 9th September, on Tower Hill, Burns remained equally uncompromising:

I tell you, lads, we will no more surrender than the men in Lucknow surrendered. . . . We are defending our Lucknow—the Lucknow of Labour. Too long have you been cooped up in the prison house of poverty, suffering, privation and disease and all the hardships of your lot. But courage! Relief is at hand. As our garrison in Lucknow, straining their eyes towards the horizon, saw the silver sheen of the bayonets of the relieving army, so from this parapet I, too, see on the horizon a silver gleam—not the gleam of bayonets to be imbrued in the blood of a brother, but the silver sheen of the full round orb of the docker's tanner.

This was the day later known as 'Black Monday'. Although money was beginning to flow in from overseas, everyone—public, employers and strikers alike—was weary of the dispute, but no end to it seemed in sight. The dock directors till refused to pay the 'tanner' before 1st January 1890; the dockers insisted on 1st October; the Lord Mayor, under pressure from Cardinal Manning, had proposed a third date, 1st December, but this was unacceptable to both sides. The

point had been reached, as so often in a major strike, when it seemed impossible that the two sides could come to terms.

But now came a ray of hope. Cardinal Manning accepted an invitation to visit Poplar and meet the whole Strike Committee, and at 5 o'clock on Tuesday September 10th, he arrived, shaking hands in turn with the sixty-five men lined up to meet him, in a schoolroom in Kirby Street, where his burly audience then squeezed themselves into school benches far too small for them. These tough, rough, unsentimental men for whom no employer held any terrors proved no match for the frail and elderly cardinal. 'He spoke to the dockers in such a quiet, firm and advising, fatherly manner', wrote Tom Mann later, 'that minute by minute, as he was speaking, one could feel the mental atmosphere changing'. Patiently and persuasively Manning urged upon them a new compromise of his own devising: an immediate return to work on the old terms, with a promise of the 'tanner' from 4th November. One by one the men who had vowed to accept nothing less than an immediate increase gave way. The first vote was 28 in favour, 14 against; the men from the Surrey side, with their separate grievances, did not vote, nor did the outsiders who had led the strike, Burns, Mann and Champion; this must be the dockers' own decision. Then Ben Tillett, who, as a dockers' delegate, had voted in the minority but immensely admired Manning, proposed that, as it had done throughout the strike, the minority should fall in with the majority's wishes. This time every hand except one (belonging to a man who had promised to oppose any compromise) was raised in Manning's support. Then, ensuring that the misunderstandings of a week earlier should not be repeated, the cardinal

Four Labour leaders

Tom Mann

John Burns

Ben Tillett

Will Thorne

obtained from the Strike Committee signed authority to negotiate on their behalf. As he left, the Irish population from the surrounding streets knelt on the pavement to seek his blessing.

But the strike was far from over. The lightermen, on the Surrey side, who had abstained in the recent vote, were demanding a separate agreement, which eventually gave them a minimum of six shillings for a twelve hour day. The dock directors at first refused to consider more concessions, but, with the strike dragging on, and ships beginning to be diverted to other ports, finally gave way. One particularly intransigent director resigned; their chief negotiator, detested by the strikers, Mr C. M. Norwood, whose plump, well-fed appearance so admirably fitted the popular image of a dock owner, was taken ill; the rest took to heart the assurance given by *The Times* that 'an inclination to listen to reason and argument' would be considered 'in the highest degree creditable to the gentlemen of Dock House'. When the dockers next met on Tower Hill it was to hear a strangely muted John Burns, talking of shaking hands with his recent adversaries who could become 'good friends, as they had been worthy foes'. At last on the afternoon of Saturday 14th September 1889, four weeks almost to the day since that first great walk-out, the agreement was signed at Dock House on the terms proposed by Manning: a minimum call-on, from 4th November, of four hours, with a two-shilling wage; and the abolition of the old 'contract' system, which would be replaced by a new one in which an elected dockers' representative allocated work in consultation with an employer's nominee. The Lord Mayor and Cardinal Manning formally witnessed the document; Ben Tillett made a speech thanking the Conciliation Committee; John Burns made a speech thanking the Lord Mayor; the Lord Mayor and the cardinal made speeches praising Burns and Tillett; then the two men rode back to Poplar on top of a cab, expecting a heroes' welcome.

They were disappointed. When the two delegates read out the details of the final agreement they were received with cries of dismay and John Burns was subjected to unprecedented heckling. It needed Ben Tillett's intervention to get the necessary victory demonstration going, with the delegates' cab being pulled in triumph to the *Wade's Arms*, though a mass victory rally in Hyde Park next day was better stage-managed.

The real hero of the hour, everyone agreed, was Cardinal Manning. A few months later he was called in again as an industrial peacemaker, in a dispute involving coalworkers, and by the time he died, two years later, his memory was venerated in the East End, while in the country he had done more to lessen anti-Catholic prejudice than any member of his faith in the sixty years since Catholic Emancipation.

Burns, his reputation and conceit higher than ever, also went on to new triumphs and, as already mentioned, to ultimate failure, at least in his followers' eyes. There was something symbolic about the fate of his famous straw hat, variously said to have been blown into the Thames on a river trip or presented to Madame Tussauds to crown Burns' effigy. It did in fact end its days ingloriously in a cupboard. The boots which Ben Tillett had worn as he tramped mile after weary mile at the head of the processions or hurried back and forth between Dock House and the *Wade's Arms* achieved a more honourable retirement. They were put on display, when they finally

GRAND OLD MANNING;

OR, THE NEW "SONG OF SIXPENCE."

SING A SONG OF SIXPENCE,
  LABOUR'S ALL AWRY;
LORD MAYOR, PRIEST, AND BISHOP
WITH FINGERS IN THE PIE;

WHEN THE PIE WAS OPENED
  THE BIRDS AT LAST DID SING,
AND THE DOCKERS GOT THEIR TAN[
THREE CHEERS FOR OLD *MANNING!*

came apart, in a shop window in the East End, as a holy relic of the great struggle.

On Monday 16th September 1889 the strikers trooped back to work. They had achieved 'the tanner' but, due to a deduction for meal times, found themselves in many cases little better off than before, while the docks now offered no living at all to those unfortunates who had turned to dock work only when all else failed, for it was now impossible to get taken on without a union card.

By November 1889 Ben Tillett's old Tea Operatives Union, with its 800 members, had grown into the Dock, Wharf, Riverside and General Labourers Union of Great Britain and Ireland, 30,000 strong, with new branches being formed almost weekly in other ports, and Tom Mann, as its first president, and Ben Tillett, as its first secretary, were already busily forming branches in other ports. Apart from being essentially a confederation of the unskilled the new union was also very different in its outlook from most of its predecessors, reared in the 'friendly society' tradition. It offered no unemployment or sick pay in return for the 2s 6d entrance fee and 2d a week subscription, but it did guarantee a 10s allowance if, or more probably when, the union called a member out on strike.

To those who had led the strike, or organised support for it outside, the Dockers' Union seemed, however, less a device for gaining more money for its members than an instrument of self and social improvement. 'We have all come out of this strike better men than we went in', claimed Poplar's M.P. Sydney Buxton. 'The men', declared John Burns, 'have gained a victory over themselves as well as over their masters. . . . The unskilled labourer, however degraded, had yet a great deal of manhood left in

him and could be raised to a higher moral and intellectual level'. In a speech delivered just before the strike ended he developed the same theme, a favourite one of his, in more detail:

Many of you will have better and higher wages than you have hitherto enjoyed. . . . You will have more steady employment. . . . When I come down to the East End of London six weeks or two months after this strike is over, I wish to see cleaner, brighter homes than I find today. . . . I shall hope to see your wives and children cleaner in person and better dressed than they are now. . . . I want to see some of your wives bear less evidence on their faces and bodies of your brutal ill-treatment. . . . I want to see when this strike is finished, some evidence of the fact that it has morally influenced you, as men, for the better. . . . I want to see you men use this strike as a new era in your personal and domestic lives. I want this strike, which has been nobly fought . . . to make a turning point in the life of the ignorant man.

The great immediate lesson of the strike, however, was of the benefits of combination. 'The wave of enthusiasm in the cause of unionism has now inundated Bristol', H. H. Champion's *Labour Elector* joyously reported six weeks after the strike in London had ended. 'Ben Tillett has been down there and received a warm welcome. . . . Swansea and Landore want branches of the union there. . . . The men of Leith are moving now. . . . They are going to combine and ask Ben Tillett and Tom Mann to go over and help them. Unionism', summed up Champion, 'means social salvation. All workers should recognise that and act upon it'. By June 1890 the D.W.R. & G.L.U., as its members were learning to call Tillett's creation, had its own *Monthly Record*, and its own emblem, 'lithographed' it was proudly said, 'in fifteen colours', which was sent to all paid-up members. This was, as this official description shows, at once a souvenir of the famous victory of 1889 and a summary of the highest aspirations of trade unionism at that time:

The central scene depicts a view taken in the London Docks, the prominent feature of which is the three-masted sailing vessel bearing the appropriate name of *Liberty,* with lighters lying alongside and a range of warehouses in the background. Entwined round its base are two sprays of oak and laurel signifying 'Stability' and 'Honour'. This is surmounted by a scroll headed 'Our Motto', containing the lines from Shelley:

> A nation made free by love, a mighty brotherhood linked by a jealous interchange of good.

Return to work

4 Class war on the Clyde

The class war is the only war worth waging.
Article in *The Socialist,* February 1916

When, in July and August 1914, the armies
of Western Europe marched off to war it was
more than the peace which was shattered.
For years the left wing parties in all the
affected countries had preached as an
article of faith that when their governments
came, as everyone foresaw they would, into
conflict, peace would be preserved by the
refusal of working men everywhere to fight
against their fellows. It was a bitter
disappointment when the 'wage-slaves'
proved no less eager for war than their
supposed oppressors.

The leader of the French Socialist Party
who, only two weeks before, had moved a
resolution calling for a general strike if war
broke out now entered the French Cabinet.
An emissary from the powerful German
Social Democratic Party, the leading
element in the Socialist International,
returned from Paris, where he had assured
his French comrades that his colleagues
would never support a war, to vote in the
Reichstag for massive war credits to the
Kaiser. The leading German Marxist,
performing a rapid intellectual somersault,
convincingly demonstrated that pure
Marxist doctrine required all good Germans
to rally against Russia, the Russian Social
Democrats being equally fervent in

championing the 'war of defence against
Prussian militarism and despotism'. In
Brussels, Keir Hardie met a group of
Labour leaders from various countries, who
duly condemned war, after which the Belgian
presiding went off to join his government
in resisting the Germans.

In London on 30th July the Parliamentary
Labour Party rejected all thought of war,
reaffirming this decision at a rally two days
later in Trafalgar Square. But within weeks
most Labour M.P.s were giving at least tacit
support to the war; within months some had
joined the Coalition government.
Everywhere the resolution passed at the
International Socialist conference held in
Basle two years before condemning
'imperialist war' was disregarded. Patriotism
proved a far more powerful force than
pleas for international brotherhood.

From the prevailing excitement only two
groups stood aloof. The future Bolsheviks,
especially Lenin safe in 'enemy' territory,
in Germany, remained unaffected by
nationalism, waiting for a greater challenge.
And in Britain, although most of the Labour
Party and its supporters rallied behind
the government, a sizeable minority,
including the chairman of the Parliamentary
Labour Party, Ramsay Macdonald, did not.
Honourably and inevitably, he resigned,
to prepare, like Lenin, for his moment,
becoming for the next four years one of
the most hated men in the country. Most

prominent left-wing and trade union leaders, however, followed what soon became the orthodox line. Many, indeed, had always insisted that patriotism and socialism were not incompatible, among them the ablest propagandist in the movement, Robert Blatchford, author of *Merrie England*, and H. M. Hyndman, founder of the first influential left-wing organisation, the Social Democratic Federation, who had, to the great disgust of many of its members, been campaigning ever since 1903 for a 'Big Navy' to stand up to Germany. Now they suddenly found themselves on the winning side. 'It seems only yesterday', observed Lenin, 'that Hyndman, having turned to the defence of imperialism . . . was looked upon by all "decent" Socialists as an unbalanced crank. . . . Now the most eminent Social Democrat leaders of all the countries have sunk to Hyndman's position'.

Only in one area of the British Isles did scepticism about the war remain strong. The vast majority of people in Scotland, as everywhere else, gave it their whole heartedsupported, but along the Clyde, in and around Glasgow, a significant and, among the working class, powerful minority, regarded it not so much with hostility as indifference.

A number of factors, some historical, some psychological, some economic, and some—if the presence of a particular individual at a particular moment can be

Glasgow street, 1914

so considered—accidental, combined to set Clydeside, or a significant minority of its population, apart from the rest of the United Kingdom in its response to the war. The city had, in 1914, a million citizens, its boundaries having been extended in 1912, thus doubling the population and bringing in a vast influx of predominantly working class voters. If the ordinary Scot prided himself on being by nature more self-assertive, if not aggressive, than his counterpart South of the Border, the Glaswegian had this combativeness to a particularly high degree. One explanation, some Scottish writers have suggested, was the presence in the city of large numbers of families of Irish, or Highland, descent, whose forebears had all, in their various ways, been victims of the landlords, and who were equally ready to resent the wealthy and high-born, for whom the employer, or the government, provided a convenient surrogate.

Significantly, although the Roman Catholic church was still officially hostile to Socialism, a Catholic Socialist Society, launched in 1906, rapidly established itself, despite the opposition of the priests, which led to its founder, John Wheatley, being denounced from the pulpit and burned in effigy by a drunken crowd. Wheatley, himself an Irishman and a miner, was one of a group of highly talented Socialist propagandists on Clydeside and later, as minister responsible for housing, became the outstanding success of the first Labour government. Equally successful, especially in appealing to the ex-Highland element in Glasgow, was a series of articles entitled *Our Noble Families*, denouncing the Scottish aristocracy, which first appeared in the Socialist magazine, *Forward*, from the pen of its owner and founder, Thomas Johnston,

who, having inherited a small printing business, had turned it into a base for anti-capitalist propaganda. *Forward* rapidly achieved a national influence and a respectable circulation of 10,000, while *Our Noble Families*, reprinted as a pamphlet, sold 100,000 copies.

Although Irish and Highlanders were largely Roman Catholic in religion another influence at work was the Calvinism in which most Scots had been reared, a religion providing many parallels to Marxism, since both offered the certainty—indeed the only hope—of salvation by working on carefully determined lines to an end already predestined. But whatever the hidden explanations, Marxism and its associated industrial movements took root more deeply, and spread more rapidly, in and round Glasgow than anywhere else in the British Isles, and most of its political 'activists' believed in conflict as a method of argument rather than conciliation. So did the industrial population. Shipyards, ports and heavy engineering plants traditionally attracted the toughest, most combative part of the working population and crowded into a ten mile long stretch along either side of the Clyde from Shettleston and Cathcart in the West to Dalmuir and Renfrew in the East were thousands of the most militant manual workers in the British Isles.

The city was unique in other ways, too. The 'gas and water Socialism' pioneered by Joseph Chamberlain in Birmingham had been even more vigorously copied beside the Clyde, which offered a wider variety of municipal enterprises than anywhere else in Britain. There was a large Labour group on the City Council—by 1902 Glasgow already had more Socialist Councillors than any other city—while the Glasgow Trades

Council, consisting of up to four hundred delegates from all the trades and industries in the area was the best organised and most powerful in the country, able to attract speakers of the calibre of Tom Mann, of Dock Strike fame.

Trade unionism, like capitalism, had come late to Scotland, but both had found that Clydeside provided fertile soil for growth. The Clyde had long been one of the world's great shipbuilding centres, but it had benefited immensely from the 'naval race' with Germany, which had more than made up for the recession in the demand for merchant ships. By 1914 a large and increasing part of the City's production

consisted of, or was connected with, warships, and this trade had brought other munitions work in its train. (Curiously enough, no-one ever seems to have suggested that if the highly-paid munition workers refused to make weapons, instead of the ill-paid soldiers to use them, all war must eventually stop.) The other great trade was heavy engineering of all kinds, with some newer additions, such as motor car and aircraft manufacture. An exceptionally high proportion of workers in these factories were skilled men and they belonged to one of the oldest-established and largest unions, the Amalgamated Society of Engineers, founded as long ago as 1851, and in 1914 by far the

Poverty in Glasgow

largest in its field, most of its members practising one of the three basic crafts of fitter, turner and machinist. On the 219,000 men organised by the four main engineering unions, almost 80%, or around 175,000, belonged to the A.S.E. Of these just under 20,000, well over 10% of the whole, were concentrated in Glasgow, spread over eight districts and thirty-one factories or shipyards, of which, by 1917, all but ten were directly concerned with some form of marine engineering or munitions work, though the rest, manufacturing such products as bridges, cranes and locomotives were hardly less important to the war effort.

The members of the A.S.E. in the various branches elected representatives to a District Committee, which had some full-time paid officials, but both delegates and officials tended to be regarded—indeed to regard themselves—as the instruments for carrying out the policy of union headquarters, rather than directly representing the local membership. On occasions disputes had been settled by head office over the heads of the local branch but it had happened even more frequently that District Committees, or individual branches, had won improvements for their members despite the lack of support from the Executive Committee in London. The tradition of local collective bargaining was well-

Shipyards on the Clyde

established by the outbreak of war and since 1892 the union had accepted the existence of shop stewards, officially appointing one or more men in each 'shop' or department of a factory or shipyard to recruit new members, pass on complaints to the District Committee and check membership cards, the union having a closed shop policy, though not always able to enforce it. The first A.S.E. shop stewards had been appointed on Clydeside in 1896, and had set up their own committee, in theory acting with the District Committee but in practice enjoying a good deal of independence, even taking part in deputations to employers and conducting negotiations over pay, especially over piecework rates involving new machines, where conditions might vary from workshop to workshop. In 1908 there had been a famous dispute on the Tyne in which the union executive had failed to prevent a strike which it had condemned and the general secretary, George Barnes, had resigned, protesting at 'an undemocratic feeling in the trade unions which worked out in the direction of the mistrust of officials'. In 1913 an even more famous dispute between the members and the executive had ended with the latter refusing to resign or leave their offices and the delegates breaking physically through the wall from the adjoining house to evict them by force. Such was the recent history of the Amalgamated Society of Engineers and by 1914 the gulf between the leadership in London and the shop stewards on the Clyde, now easily the union's most turbulent and disobedient area, could hardly have been wider.

Launching a ship

Although the city had in the past been traditionally Liberal, and tolerant, in its politics, the situation was by 1914 changing rapidly. The prevailing climate, at least among the more active political leaders and especially in the larger trade unions, was becoming increasingly left-wing, and largely Marxist, with some under-currents of syndicalism, favouring the ownership of individual plants and industries by their work-force, and even of anarchism. Probably the prevailing temper was one of automatic disagreement. 'The Clydesiders', whether on their native heath or later in Parliament, felt more at home in opposition, than when supporting authority of any kind. By far the largest left-wing political organisation in Scotland was the Independent Labour Party, which, in Scotland, *was* the Labour Party, though far more progressive, as it would have called itself, than its opposite number, and nominal ally, in England. In Glasgow, however, it counted as moderate and in terms of members it outnumbered its two rivals for popular support by ten to one. The I.L.P. was fortunate in attracting a number of able, eloquent and intensely admired leaders, like the future Labour M.P. James Maxton, then a young schoolmaster newly converted to Socialism, the housing specialist, John Wheatley, already described, and the tough and vigorous Emmanuel Shinwell, the son of a Jewish clothes dealer, who had worked in a 'Co-op' shop before becoming President of the Trades Council and taking on, in his twenties—he was 30 in 1914—the notoriously difficult job of organising a union among the merchant seamen on Clydeside, his qualifications including his

Shipyard workers

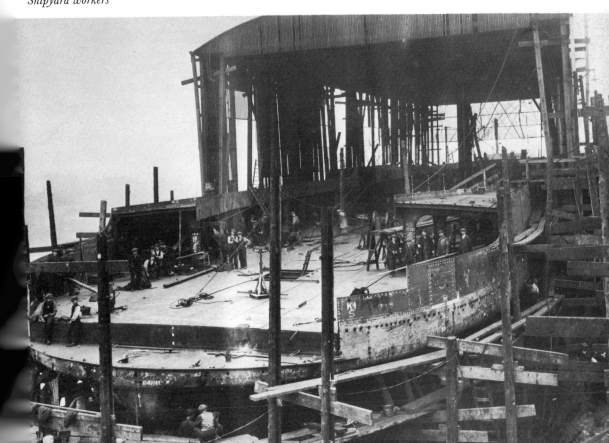

reputation as an amateur boxer. He had been so successful that, after a national strike in 1911, he had succeeded in getting better terms for his men than any other negotiator in the country.

Also in the I.L.P., though at various times also belonging to other parties further to the left, was another future M.P., David Kirkwood, who, after leaving school at twelve, had had a variety of odd jobs, such as errand boy, before becoming a skilled engineer. He had worked in various engineering plants all over Clydeside before, so he claimed, becoming known as 'Kirkwood of Parkhead', after taking a job in the great Parkhead Forge owned by Sir William Beardmore. This, since 1910, had been turning out heavy weapons for the new battleships, and according to Kirkwood, a man proud of his trade and its 'beautiful machinery', contained the finest gun-shop in the world. By April 1914 Kirkwood, now aged 43, was the leading figure in the Parkhead Branch of the Amalgamated Society of Engineers, and that month took the step which was to make him well-known throughout the union, demanding a twopence an hour increase. The proposal was described as ridiculous by the union's chairman, who said that a reasonable rise would be a farthing an hour, and Kirkwood's claim, which would have carried the men's basic wages from 38s 3d a week to 47s 7d, was still unsettled at the outbreak of war.

In a somewhat similar position to Kirkwood, ('I was already', he wrote of this period, 'well known as a revolutionary agitator'), was another Clydesider soon to be associated with him in the public mind, though there was in fact little love lost between the two men, William Gallacher, later one of the only two Communist M.P.s ever to sit in the House of Commons.

Gallacher united in his ancestry both the threads of 'rebel' influence which had shaped Clydeside, his father being an Irishman and his mother a Highlander, and, like Kirkwood, Gallacher, had started work as a grocer's boy at the age of twelve before staging a one-man strike, against excessive work, which was a complete success. Later, as a merchant seaman on the Atlantic run, he staged another and this time also got his money, but lost his job. By the outbreak of war Gallacher, aged 32, was already disillusioned with the I.L.P., considering that it 'smacked too much of the Sunday school', and was a shop steward in the Albion Motor Works, Glasgow's only surviving motor car plant, soon to be classed as a 'war factory' when it turned over to making vehicles for the Army.

Most of the leading left-wingers on Clydeside had at one time or another belonged to one of the Marxist organisations outside the I.L.P., which, though numbering their supporters only in hundreds, exerted a wide influence. The most important were the Socialist Labour Party, which had broken away from the Social Democratic Federation in 1903, and the British Socialist Party, founded following a further seccession in 1905. Gallacher belonged to the British Socialist Party and Kirkwood to the Socialist Labour Party, but such nominal allegiances were not important, since the real political division on Clydeside was between those who believed in parliamentary and constitutional methods to transform society and those who looked to a not-too-distant revolution, to be achieved as much by direct action by the working class as by political means.

In the years before the war the great apostle of Marxism in Scotland, and especially on Clydeside, had been a

David Kirkwood

William Gallacher

John Mclean

Sir William Beardmore

dedicated young schoolmaster, John Maclean, whom most people in England had never heard of, and who never reached Parliament, but who was singled out for praise by Lenin. Gallacher, one of his converts, considered Maclean to be 'certainly the greatest revolutionary figure that Scotland ever produced', while David Kirkwood thought him 'as sincere as sunlight, and as passionate as a typhoon'. The son of a pottery worker, and grandson of a displaced Highlander, Maclean had been reared on tales of ancient grievances. 'His maternal grandmother', wrote Maclean's daughter and biographer, 'used to take "wee Johnnie" on her knee and tell him how the wicked landlords had taken the farms and crofts of the poor people of the north' and from 1900, when, at the age of twenty one, he qualified as a teacher and rejected religion, his whole life was dedicated to denouncing capitalism and war. '*Merrie England*', declared Maclean, 'is the primary school of Socialism but *Das Kapital* is the university' and once he had embraced Marxism his dedication to it never wavered. Every spare moment, including all the long school holidays, Maclean spent stumping the country and especially Clydeside, preaching the gospel of revolution and conducting huge classes in economics and history from a strictly Marxist point of view. Far better educated than most of his hearers, Maclean had the eloquence and fervour of an Old Testament prophet and the dedication of a saint: his early death from pneumonia, at the age of 44 in 1923, followed his insistence on addressing outdoor meetings all through a bitter Winter, though already ill, after giving his overcoat to a friend. 10,000 people followed his coffin to its grave, and however controversial his views, of their impact in moulding opinion,

especially before 1914, there can be no question.

The Summer of 1914 was a fine and hot one in Glasgow, as everywhere else, though its most politically-conscious citizens had more on their minds than wondering how to make the most of the weather. 'In July 1914; explained Gallacher later, 'the shop stewards . . . went off for their annual Summer holidays, determined on their return to make the engineering shops 100 per cent trade union in preparation for the struggle that lay ahead in November', the 'struggle' being to secure the extra twopence an hour already demanded at Parkhead by David Kirkwood, which 'meant 8s extra in wages for the 54 hour week' and November being the date on which the existing agreement expired.

On August Bank Holiday war was declared and long before November the whole situation had changed. With the nation crying out for arms the men's bargaining position became immeasurably more powerful, but at the same time the mood of both government and public was far less sympathetic to demands for higher wages. So, too, was the trade union movement as a whole. The T.U.C. had immediately pledged its support to the war and, three weeks after it had begun, an 'industrial truce' was proclaimed by the leading unions. The Executive Committee of the Amalgamated Society of Engineers, the dominant union on Clydeside, even, on 17th September, recommended its members to assist in recruiting men for the Army, though in the face of protests it later withdrew this advice.

If the reaction of their leaders, and of the Labour Party, had disappointed the militants on Clydeside what followed shocked them even more. In a spontaneous outburst of patriotism working men from all over the country hurried to enlist and nowhere was the response more enthusiastic than in the two heavy engineering areas of South Wales and Clydeside and in the engineering industry generally, from which, by June 1915, one in five male workers had volunteered. The cause of this 'evil plague' of 'war fever', decided William Gallacher, was 'The wild excitement, the illusion of wonderful adventure and the actual break in the deadly monotony of working class life. Thousands went flocking to the colours in the first days, not because of any "love of country", not because of any high feeling of "patriotism" but because of the new, strange and thrilling life that lay before them'. Whatever the volunteers' motives, however, the response on Clydeside was enormous and, as the war memorial which now stands in George Square, Glasgow proudly proclaims, no fewer than 200,000 people—volunteers and conscripts—went from Glasgow to serve in the Forces between 1914 and 1918, out of 8 million from the whole Empire, so that one serviceman in every forty was a Glaswegian, a truly remarkable figure.

There is no memorial in George Square to another record to which Glasgow could lay claim, that of containing far more people actively opposed to the first world war than any other city in the British Isles. Nowhere else in the country could John Maclean have contained in safety to denounce the war on street corners, nowhere else could Ramsay MacDonald have been given, as Gallacher claims he was, 'a great reception' at a crowded meeting. Gallacher did not think much of his visitor's politics but 'the press

Volunteers in George Square, Glasgow, August 1914

Down with the strikers!

Down with the bosses!

had made him appear as a great figure against the war, so Glasgow was prepared to give him a welcome', with 'shop stewards brought in to protect the meeting' and Gallacher and Shinwell both appearing on the platform. (Also present was the future I.L.P. Member of Parliament, John McGovern, who, though a pacifist, had come equipped to protect the speaker with a 'short, heavy piece of lead pipe' prompting MacDonald's wry comment: 'That's the sort of pacifist I like to see'.) In contrast to what happened elsewhere, it was often, in Glasgow, pro-war hecklers who were in danger at anti-war meetings. 'There were patriots in Glasgow all right', admitted Gallacher, 'but somehow they never could get going. Meetings were attempted but these generally ended up in demonstrations against the war'. A Glasgow branch of the newly-formed Scottish Patriotic League, founded to 'finish the pacifists' achieved nothing except to land its founder in hospital, while a local branch of the Discharged and Demobilised Soldiers' and Sailors' Federation—consisting largely of men too badly wounded for further service—merely provided more recruits for the anti-war movement. By contrast even the legendary Ben Tillett, hero of the Dock Strike, but now described by Gallacher as 'the first of the big "Defend our country" demagogues to visit Glasgow', was 'hooted off the platform'.

The 'pro-war' and 'anti-war' division polarised political opinion on the Clyde and helped to complete the sense of alienation of many working men from their party and union leadership. Ten of the Independent Labour M.P.s signed a defence of the war in October 1914, while the bulk of their supporters in Scotland remained instinctively, if not openly, 'internationalist'

and pacifist, resulting in such curious compromises as editions of *Forward* in which patriotic appeals appeared alongside equally eloquent denunciations of 'the capitalists' war'.

The *Socialist*, organ of the Socialist Labour Party (which also, however, suffered from divisions until the last 'imperialists' were driven from it in 1916), offered counsel even more acceptable on Clydeside. 'Should the Socialist Party', it asked in February 1916, 'pretend that all is well with the world because the capitalists have organised a gigantic murder feast? . . . If the Socialist party does that it is committing suicide. . . . The class war is the only war worth waging'.

The campaign against the war began on its first Sunday, August 10th, when John Maclean thundered against it in Glasgow, while William Gallacher organised a similar demonstration in his native Paisley, and in a public debate a few weeks later—which could have been held at this time nowhere but in Scotland—he put the classic Marxist point of view:

The adversity of the capitalist class is the opportunity of the working class. Let us take advantage of it and go forward for a victory, not for the imperialist allies, but for the working class.

The leading militants rejected even the middle position adopted by some members of the essentially Marxist Socialist Labour Party, who argued that, while refusing to take part in foreign wars, a man could properly defend his own country. 'The workers have no country', shouted David Kirkwood, when the editor of *The Socialist* advanced this argument in one debate, and walked out there and then to join the I.L.P. The famous question 'What did you do in the Great War, daddy?' often received on Clydeside a cynical answer. 'My boy', a rent-factor—i.e. landlord's agent—was supposed to have said, 'I did munition workers'. Even the classic 'Kitchener Wants You' poster often attracted a derisory postscript:

Your King and Country Need You
Ye hardy sons of toil,
But will your King and Country need you
When they're sharing out the spoil?

The shop stewards' attitude was prompted partly by pacifism—though Kirkwood himself declared 'The country must win'—partly by the desire to seize the political opportunities presented by the war, but most of all by a determination to protect and consolidate their members' craft privileges.

It probably found a wider response than it would otherwise have done due to the rising cost of living, which, ironically, hit soldiers' families particularly hard: Army allowances to dependants were scandalously small and often slow in arriving. Prices began to climb as soon as the war began, and though detailed records for individual items were not at first kept by the government, by December 1914 the official index of retail food prices, 100 in July, had already risen to 116; by February 1915 it was 122, by December 1915, 144. Other costs, of rent, clothes, household equipment (a scrubbing brush costing 7d in 1914 was 1s 2d by 1919, and a 11d bucket had soared to 5s 6d) also

Fitting a naval gun

rose sharply, while the most popular of luxuries, beer, due to wartime taxation, went up from 3d a pint on the outbreak of war to 4d in November and later to 5d. Higher prices seemed to lend support to the militants' charges that the 'boss class' were making a good thing out of the war and that every good trade unionist should fight them at every opportunity, with or without his union's approval.

While the shop stewards saw in the nation's emergency a unique opportunity to improve their members' position, some employers, too, also felt that it provided a chance not to be missed of reasserting proper discipline in industry. Concern about the growing power and arrogance of the shop stewards had been increasing on Clydeside even before the war. 'Had the war not intervened', wrote the general manager of G. & J. Weir and Co's works at Cathcart, 'the Autumn of 1914 would probably have seen an industrial disturbance of the first magnitude'. The firm had become particularly exasperated by the restrictive practices of the engineering unions, which hindered the introduction of new and more elaborate machines, able to convert work 'which had formerly demanded the judgement and dexterity of the skilled man' to quote the historians of the Clyde's war effort, 'into a series of more or less repetitive operations', easily mastered in 'a few weeks'. Weirs' works had long been a battle-ground of demarcation disputes and arguments over whether one man should be allowed to supervise more than one machine, while the unions steadily refused to allow unskilled or semi-skilled men to carry out operations traditionally done by their members, even where the employment of craftsmen had become an expensive anachronism. Also weary of interference in

management by his manual workers was Sir William Beardmore who, a little later in his great Parkhead works, remarked to the chairman of his shop stewards, (who took the comment as a joke): 'Look here, Kirkwood, are these your works or mine?'

By December 1914 the Glasgow District of the Amalgamated Society of Engineers had already given the shop stewards (whom the union's Executive in London heartily distrusted, as a threat to their own authority) an official status, as a 'vigilance committee' designated to watch developments in the workshops on their behalf, and that month the claim first proposed in June, for a 2d an hour increase for all skilled A.S.E. members working on Clydeside was formally submitted. Even without the unlimited overtime available to munition workers, it would have put the Clydeside engineers nearly 9s a week ahead of most others in the British Isles and 6s 1d a week of those in Sheffield, then the union's best paid area, though Gallacher declared (with obvious exaggeration) that even 6d an hour would hardly have compensated for the rise in the cost of living.

The employers, however, responded to the claim by offering only three farthings an hour, and, while a ballot was being held among A.S.E. membership throughout the West of Scotland, during January a ban on overtime was introduced in one engineering works on Clydeside after another, the first serious industrial action of the war.

No-one was more infuriated by what seemed to him this cynical attempt to bargain with men's lives, since both the Royal Navy and the Army depended on the factories of the Clyde, than William Weir, the 37 year old head of W. J. Weir and Co, whose firm owed its existence to the skill and enterprise of his father, an engineer,

Sir William Weir

a thinly veiled attack on his own employees. 'Every hour lost by a workman which COULD HAVE been worked', wrote Weir, 'HAS been worked by a German workman, who in that time has produced, say, an additional shell . . . to kill the British workman's brother-in-arms, or perhaps a bomb to be dropped on his wife and children'.

The last straw, from the men's point of view, was the introduction by Weir's due to the shortage of skilled tradesmen in Scotland, of thirty skilled turners and fitters from America, who, according to the shop stewards, though the company denied this, were being paid six shillings a week more than their British workmates. This precipitated a strike of 2,000 men on 16th February 1915, for the company possessed what William Gallacher described as 'one of the best organised shops in Glasgow, with a fine body of shop stewards'. The shop stewards at the Albion Motor Works, Gallacher's own factory, instantly brought their men out in support, and Gallacher addressed a crowded meeting of the strikers:

I said that I brought greetings from the Albion and a pledge of solidarity so long as the fight lasted. I told them Yarrow's (shipbuilders and marine engineers of Scotstoun) and Meechan's (engaged on 'munitions and general' engineering) were on the move and that before the day was out we would have the whole of Clydeside closed down. What a scene there was as they jumped to their feet and cheered! . . . What an inspiration it was to them. And what an inspiration they were to the other delegates now arriving from the other factories, at the hall. . . . By the evening all the principal factories had decided. The great Clyde Strike of February 1915 was on.

Gallacher later insisted that the strike was 'spontaneous' not 'unofficial' since it included 'branch officials, district officials

who had invented various improved processes for ships' engines and built up the business until it was the leading manufacturer of marine pumping equipment and condensers and a major contractor to the Admiralty. Out of pure patriotism—it was outside their normal field and they planned to give all profits to the Red Cross and similar charities—Weirs began as early as October 1914 to plan to go into shell production but although the shell shortage was already notorious, he encountered, complained William Weir, 'every day endless trouble'. Weir consolidated his unpopularity with the militants, and they confirmed his contempt for them, when the usual Hogmanay celebrations were followed by heavy absenteeism. Only 1% of the workforce turned up at Weir's Cathcart factory on Monday 4th January 1915 and only 25—50% next day, prompting him to issue a pamphlet, *Responsibility and Duty* which was and . . . executive officials (like myself)', and 'to escape the threats of the Defence of the Realm Act', passed in August 1914 and later strengthened, 'we formed, instead of a "Strike Committee, a "Labour-Witholding" Committee, with myself as Chairman and J. M. Messer'—the leading shop steward at Weir's—'as secretary'. The government, the T.U.C., and above all the general public were in no mood, however, for such semantic niceties:

The press shrieked for action against the leaders; everywhere in the ranks of the bourgeoisie and petty-bourgeoisie we were cursed and condemned. Of all the multitude of press organs, with the exception of one or two weeklies with very small circulations there was no one to say a word for us. . . . Travelling round the area in tram or train you could hear the strike discussed. Shopkeepers and small business men were venomous. 'The leaders should be shot'. 'It's obvious they're in the pay of the Germans.' 'This man Maclean is the cause of all the trouble; why don't they lock him up?' . . . 'This Gallacher, I understand he's just a drunken blackguard. . . .' As day followed day and the strike continued the attacks on us became terrific.

The 8,000 men on strike were unmoved by the hostile reaction of their fellow-citizens and two officials from the Executive Committee of the Amalgamated Society of Engineers, who addressed a meeting of the leaders at the Palace Theatre, Glasgow, on Friday 19th February 1915, had a rough reception, one of them being interrupted

Mass meeting at Weir's factory

and the other refused a hearing. The meeting then passed, the *Glasgow Herald* reported, 'a unanimous resolution in favour of remaining out until the advance of 2d per hour was granted'; the immediate grievance, of the American engineers, had now been swept up into the larger one, about pay. It was clear, too, that it was not merely a few 'agitators' who were involved. The result of a ballot on the employers' offer of three farthings, announced at this moment, showed an eleven to one majority against acceptance. The voting in Glasgow alone was even more overwhelming, 6,439 to 594.

Since the strike was unofficial no-one was receiving a penny in strike pay and it was probably a relief to the organisers, when' they were able, after three weeks, to persuade the men to return. The strike was settled (not without some mutterings alleging a 'sell out') by David Kirkwood, always something of an odd man out on such occasions, who agreed to a compromise proposed by the Board of Trade of an increase of 1d an hour. Although this was only half what they were asking and only one farthing an hour more than they could have got without striking, Gallacher was probably right to claim the result was a victory for the Shop Stewards, and it was certainly a defeat for the union leadership who had refused to support the strikers and had advised acceptance of the employers' original offer. He afterwards wrote:

It was a great strike. The loyalty and solidarity of the workers could not have been higher. The organisation and contacts between the factories and the areas and between the areas and the centre was almost perfect. It ended, not on a note of defeat, but with a feeling of something achieved. The workers of the Clyde had broken through the rotten atmosphere of war-jingoism and stood out, strong and unafraid, ready to defend their class against their class enemies.

The lesson of the shop stewards' success was not lost on the employers. At the Parkhead works, where new employees were now flooding in, and the A.S.E. members, Sir William Beardmore complained, were 'hindering the strangers and making it difficult for them . . . because they are not in the union', the management capitulated completely, agreeing to establish a closed shop and giving Kirkwood the right to move freely about the works, to resolve grievances on the spot, and to appeal if necessary to Sir William himself. 'David Kirkwood stalks about the works as if they were not mine but his', his employer later remarked, and to Kirkwood's description of himself as a 'slave' he retorted that '"dictator" would be a better word'.

With the widespread adoption of the closed shop, either with the employers' co-operation or their tacit agreement, for the sake of industrial peace, membership of the Amalgamated Society of Engineers soared. In the East End district of Glasgow, containing Parkhead, it rose by 25% during the war, compared to 63% (to 19,931) over Glasgow as a whole. Meanwhile, however, the gulf between the union leadership and the militants on Clydeside widened. In March along with other unions, the Amalgamated Society of Engineers officially agreed to accept the suspension of traditional trade union rules and practices in return for government limitation of profits, but this made little difference on Clydeside, as by May, William Weir was publicly complaining in the *Glasgow Herald*:

Every possible opportunity is seized to put forward claims for higher wages, advantage is taken of every innovation on an employer's part . . . to make it a basis for further demands, until the position has become so difficult that an employer has really to consider whether he should . . . take on government work of a new nature . . . in case he involves himself in labour difficulties, which will affect his entire business. . . .

Reports of enormously high wages being earned on shipbuilding and repair work—£5–£6 a week was said, in a special report prepared for the Home Office in April 1915, to be common, and £10–£15 not unknown—and reports of widespread drunkenness, and associated absenteeism, holding up vital production there, increased public irritation with the men on the Clyde. The drinking problem in industrial areas was tackled by the Liquor Control Act, passed in May, though the shop stewards could in any case hardly be blamed; the left-wing contained a strong temperance element and both Gallacher and Kirkwood were teetotallers. Far more important was the creation in the same month of the coalition government, which included the leader of the Parliamentary Labour Party, Arthur Henderson, and a new post, Minister of Munitions, filled by David Lloyd George, the ablest and most dynamic figure in the government.

The new Minister set out his policy in a speech on 3rd June in which he warned that 'we must increase the mobility of labour and . . . have greater subordination in labour to the direction and control of the state'. The voluntary agreement which he had made with the unions while still at the Treasury was now given the force of law in the Munitions Act, which reached the statute book on 3rd July. It had four main provisions. Strikes on war work became illegal and arbitration compulsory. A War Munitions Volunteers Scheme, already in force on the Clyde, under which skilled men could volunteer to be sent wherever they were needed, was given the force of law.

Restrictive practices were banned in 'controlled establishments', engaged on munitions manufacture, in return for an undertaking to restore them after the war and to control profits; and it was made illegal to take on 'a workman who has within the last previous six weeks . . . been employed on . . . munitions work' unless he could produce 'a leaving certificate' confirming that he had left his last job with his employer's consent. This last provision was designed to prevent 'poaching', by which key men, trading on their scarcity value, might be tempted away by higher wages to another, perhaps less essential job; but at a time when there was still no conscription and no general direction of labour, it infuriated militants like David Kirkwood:

The outstanding feature of the Munitions Act was that it denied the men the right to sell their labour to the highest bidder . . . and to the men of Clydeside it appeared little short of slavery. . . . I felt it like that. I was happy in Beardmore's as a free man. I resented being in Beardmore's as a slave. . . . The Clyde's reply to the Munitions Act was the Clyde Workers Committee.

The Committee did not in fact come into existence at once, though that Summer there were rumblings of discontent on Clydeside. In June a shop steward at Beardmore's was sent to prison for assault after trying to enforce a restrictive practice on a reluctant workmate but serious trouble was averted when the union, by 'backstairs diplomacy', managed to secure his release. In August, when two men were sacked from Fairfields shipyard in Govan for 'slacking', 430 shipwrights went on strike in protest and to their great astonishment, the seventeen shop stewards responsible found themselves being fined £10 each, with the option of thirty days in jail. The strike was broken,

2.

Clyde Workers' Committee

TO ALL CLYDE WORKERS

FELLOW-WORKERS,

Since the outbreak of the European War, many changes have been brought about of vital interest to the workers. Foremost amongst these has been the **scrapping** of Trade Union Rules, and the consequent undermining of the whole Trade Union Movement. To the intelligent workers it has been increasingly clear that the officials have failed to grasp the significance of these changes, and as a result have been unable to formulate a policy that would adequately protect the interests of those workers whom they are supposed to represent.

The support given to the Munitions Act by the Officials was an act of Treachery to the Working Class. Those of us who refused to be **Sold** have organized the above Committee, representative of **All Trades** in the Clyde area, determined to retain what liberties we have, and to take the first opportunity of forcing the repeal of all the pernicious legislation that has recently been imposed upon us. In the words of a Manifesto issued by the Trade Union Rights Committee, recently formed in London :—

" Let us preserve what rights still remain and refuse steadfastly to surrender another inch to our allied foes—the capitalists and politicians. The liberty and freedom of the organized worker is the one thing; our fight is the fight that matters, and now is the time to act."

WHAT THE COMMITTEE IS AND ITS PURPOSE.

It is composed of Delegates or Shop Stewards from all Trades in the Glasgow area, and is open to all such *bona fide* workers. The progressives in all Trades are invited to attend. Its origin goes back to the last big strike of February, 1915, when action was taken to force the

[P. T. O.

demand put forward for an increase of 2d. per hour in the Engineering industry. At that time a Committee known as the **Labour With-holding Committee** was set up, representative of the different Trades in the industry, to organise the strike, and notwithstanding the fierce opposition from public opinion, employers, Government, and **our own officials** alike, that Committee managed and carried through probably the best organised strike in the annals of Clyde history, and brought about closer working unity amongst the rank and file of the different Trades than years of official effort. It became obvious then that such a Committee permanently established would be valuable workers, and with that purpose in view the Committee was kept in being after the termination of the strike.

Recently, when the three Govan shipwrights were locked up under the Munitions Act, many appeals were sent to the Committee to again take action. In answer to those appeals the Committee called its forces together and discussed certain lines of action, and, despite all reports to the contrary, it was through "the powers that be" getting to know that the Committee was again at work, that ultimately forced the release of the three shipwrights.

At this juncture it was considered advisable to change the name of this body, and from now on it will be known as the **Clyde Workers' Committee (C.W.C.).**

Our purpose must not be misconstrued, we are out for unity and closer organisation of all trades in the industry, one Union being the ultimate aim. We will support the officials just so long as they rightly represent the workers, but we will act independently immediately they misrepresent them. Being composed of Delegates from every shop, and untrammelled by obselete rule or law, we claim to represent the true feeling of the workers. We can act immediately according to the merits of the case and the desire of the rank and file.

The following Trades are at present represented on the Committee. All other Trades are kindly invited to become attached. All Shop Stewards welcome :—A.S.E., Toolmakers, Boilermakers, Blacksmiths, Shipwrights, Coppersmiths, Brassfinishers, Patternmakers, Miners, Tinsmiths, Sheet-iron Workers, Electrical Trades, Joiners, Gas and **General Workers**, School Teachers, Coopers.

For further information see your Shop Steward. Speakers will be sent on request to Work Gates, Districts, and generally be at the convenience of the workers.

Signed on behalf of the Committee,

WM. GALLACHER, President.

J. M. MESSER, Secretary,
408 Allison Street.

but memories of the incident festered and on 12th September 1915 the Shop Stewards Vigilance Committee, chaired by David Kirkwood, passed a resolution demanding the repeal of the 'Slave Clauses' of the Munitions Act. On 30th September, the General Secretary of the A.S.E., attempting to defend them, was shouted down at a meeting of rank and file members who clamoured to hear their two heroes, David Kirkwood and James Messer instead.

Since the 'twopenny strike' which they had led in February Kirkwood (of Beardmore's, Parkhead) Messer (of Weir's), Gallacher (of Albion) and other leading shop stewards had kept in touch through regular, if unofficial meetings, and this loose organisation was now made more formal. On Saturday 2nd October 1915 a meeting of delegates from engineering and shipbuilding works all over Clydeside, under David Kirkwood's chairmanship, voted to set up a 'strong representative committee' designed 'to organise the prevailing opposition to the operation of this Act' this body being known as the Clyde Trades Vigilance Committee, and drawing its power from similar committees in the factories. One of its first acts was to demand the release of three shipwrights still in jail, and they were soon afterwards set free, after the union had secretly paid their fines; but this sort of concealed, though effective, action was despised by the real militants, who were spoiling for a public confrontation with the law, and at the end of October 1915 the Vigilance Committee, more powerful than ever, was renamed the Clyde Workers Committee. Its members set out their philosophy in a stirring leaflet:

We will support the officials just so long as they rightly represent the workers, but we will act independently immediately they misrepresent them. Being composed of delegates from every shop and untrammelled by obsolete rule or law, we claim to represent the true feelings of the workers. We can act immediately according to the merits of the case and the desire of the rank and file.

The committee had no written constitution but at once began to hold meetings every Saturday in a hall in Ingram Street, where 250 to 300 delegates assembled drawn from the mine-workers, railwaymen and co-operative society employees in the areas, as well as from the engineering unions, especially the A.S.E. which provided its main strength. The Committee was distinct from previous union organisations in the variety of trades it represented and in the way in which each workshop, not each union branch, had its own delegates, though they seem to have 'emerged' rather than been chosen by formal election. The key members, who formed an inner cabinet meeting separately twice a week, were all shop stewards involved in the February strike and all Marxists or near-Marxists. The secretary was James Messer of Weir's the chairman, James Gallacher, of Albion, and a leading member (in his own eyes *the* leading member) was David Kirkwood, of Beardmore's forge at Parkhead.

Most significantly, the Committee united unions jealous in the past of each other's power. William Gallacher, for example, was a 'brassie', or member of the United Brassfounders Association, which had formerly negotiated only in alliance with such comparatively minor unions as those representing the boilermakers and pattern-makers, the giant A.S.E. having pursued its own course, so that sometimes both were, quite independently, making the same demand to the same employers at the same time. Now for the first time all the militants on Clydeside, irrespective of relations between their individual unions at national level, joined together in forging and carrying out a common policy. For members of the Amalgamated Society of Engineers, who had in the past been described by their envious colleagues as 'the blue blood of the working class', it was an act of condescension to co-operate with lesser brethren, speedily vindicated by the increased power which all those involved now found they possessed. It was this, as much as the essentially undemocratic views of its members—the left-wing *Herald* had described the leaders of the February strike as having 'kept the flag of revolutionary trade unionism flying'—which gave the Clyde Workers Committee its special importance.

To the official union leadership, to the military authorities on the Clyde, and to the government in London, the Committee must have looked like the standard bearer of revolution and its activities firmly established the legend of the 'Red Clyde'. Contrary to popular belief, however, it was not an intrinsically anti-war body, although it did at first include at least two revolutionaries who had no connection with industry, John Maclean and his Russian associate and lodger, Peter Petrov, whose mere name, nationality and background—he had been driven out of Czarist Russia for Communist activities—were enough to alarm all sober citizens. Both eventually left the Committee after failing to turn it into a 'stop the war' movement and after indulging in some distinctly unfraternal intrigues against their colleagues. Maclean, as will be described later, ended up in jail for sedition, Petrov joined the Russian Foreign Service after the Russian revolution, only to flee back to England, several years

later, for the second time, to seek the protection of the 'capitalist tyranny' he had so often denounced.

The activities of Maclean and Petrov apart, the Committee's first opportunity to attract public attention came in November on, from its point of view, an ideal issue. Housing on Clydeside had always been exceptionally bad and, by November 1915 rents had risen, due to the general increase in costs and the influx of new workers, by as much as 12–23%, leading to a rent strike by many tenants, including some soldiers' families. The landlords countered with the threat of eviction for those who refused to pay and on 17th November summoned eighteen tenants before the Small Debts Court, which could order the deduction of the arrears owed from their wages. On the morning of the hearing 15,000 people, many drawn from the shipyards and munitions factories, swarmed round the courthouse, where a deputation bluntly told the presiding Sheriff: 'These men will only resume work in the event of you deciding against the factors; if you do not, it means that the workers on the lower reaches will stop work tomorrow and join them'. It was manifestly not a constitutional protest, but it worked. After consulting the Ministry of Munitions in London the Sherriff refused to make an order for payment and next day the government announced that it was bringing in a Bill to freeze rents at their July 1914 level. The Clyde Workers Committee had not organised the rent strike, nor, as Gallacher falsely claimed, had it succeeded in bringing a single factory to a halt on the day of the court proceedings, but it gained most of the credit from the result. This initial success also encouraged it to further defiance. As a military intelligence officer keeping watch on the 'disaffected' Clyde reported to London, the militants clearly felt that 'as they got the better of the government over rents, by intimidation, they will be able to do the same thing over the Munitions Act'.

Although it was the 'leaving certificate', (later abandoned by the government), which had provoked the initial outburst of fury against the Act on the Clyde, the Committee realised that a far more serious long-term threat to it now came from the Ministry's policy of 'dilution', which meant bringing in and training new workers, including women, to do jobs hitherto reserved for skilled craftsmen. The union leadership had accepted dilution, as part of their pact with the government, on the understanding that their members did not lose by it and that the 'dilutees' disappeared

after the war, and it had up to now caused little trouble, since it had mainly been confined to shell manufacture, a new trade for the area and one likely to cease at the end of the war. But the introduction of unskilled men, and women new to factory work, to undertake engineers' work in existing plants was another matter, and resistance on the Clyde seemed likely to be so serious that Lloyd George, persuaded against his better judgement by his labour colleague, Arthur Henderson, agreed late in December 1915 to visit the area in person to explain why the nation's need required the surrender of their most cherished privileges.

Lloyd George no doubt hoped that his famous charm and eloquence, linked to his reputation as a champion of the working

Women operating milling machines, 1914–18 War

man, for whom he had done more than any living politician, would win over even the tough strike-hardened craftsmen of the Clyde, but the visit began under unhappy auspices. First it was 'on', then 'off', then 'on' again, the problem being that, out of loyalty to the union leaders, on whose support the government depended, the Minister was unwilling to meet the Clyde Workers Committee, while without their co-operation he could hardly reach their followers.

He hoped to solve the dilemma by meeting them individually, as shop stewards in their various factories or in their capacity of elected union officials, but was easily outmanoeuvred by Gallacher and the rest. The members of the Committee planned to present a united front against Lloyd George, by refusing to welcome him into their factories, or to meet him individually, though this was broken by David Kirkwood, who was flattered by a personal telegram delivered to him at Parkhead. ('The great man', remarked Sir William Beardmore good naturedly, in passing it on, 'is coming to see you, not me'.) But the occasion provided a bad beginning to what was supposed to be a triumphal tour. Lloyd George was late—giving Kirkwood the chance to score a neat point: 'Does he no' ken there's a war on?' he asked, 'We're here to produce munitions'—and when the two finally met Kirkwood introduced him to his fellow shop-stewards in a speech of memorable ungraciousness: 'Every word you say will be carefully weighed. We regard you with suspicion because the Munitions Act with which your name is associated has the taint of slavery about it'. The Act, had, said Kirkwood, 'bound the workers to Beardmore as completely as if it had branded "B" on their brows', suiting the action to

the word by tracing out the letter on his forehead. Against such histrionics even Lloyd George's magic proved unavailing and his plea to the shop stewards to remember their 'brothers in the trenches' fell on stony ground.

Later that evening, Arthur Henderson, the chief organiser of the tour, had an even more discouraging reception from William Gallacher, who treated him to a long diatribe against the Munitions Act, before those present voted overwhelmingly to send the leader of the Labour Party 'back with a message to his master that the Clyde trade unionists are not the lackeys of the workers' enemies'. The shop stewards then went home in style at the nation's expense; as a joke, Gallacher had said that he and his union colleagues would only meet Henderson if taxis were provided to take them home, and these now duly arrived. There was a further disastrous encounter next day when Lloyd George, reluctantly discussing with the shop stewards plans for the coming conference, was treated to a lecture, as Gallacher recorded, by one of his supporters, Arthur MacManus:

We knew it was a war for trade and territory, said MacManus, a war carried on for the purposes of imperialism. We were not supporting any such war. We opposed it. Therefore, there was no possibility of getting us to yield in the slightest degree on any issue affecting conditions in the industry, by any appeal based on the need for winning the war. If that were understood, we should be in a better position to face the only question before us: 'Who is going to control dilution?'

The Committee made their demands even more clear in two blunt exchanges with their distinguished visitor. 'Who's going to control the factories?', asked Kirkwood rhetorically. 'I tell you, Mr Lloyd George, Minister of Munitions, we are'. And for the first time they stated plainly their demand for nationalisation of industry, to which Lloyd George replied that 'It would mean a revolution and you can't carry through a revolution in the midst of a war'.

Finally, on the morning of Saturday 25th December 1915, the long-planned face-to-face confrontation between the most formidable—and perhaps already the most powerful—minister in the British government and the recalcitrant shop stewards and militant manual workers of Clydeside at last took place. The Clyde Workers Committee had, in the end secured most of the tickets and the occasion which followed was not one which anyone present ever forgot, least of all David Kirkwood:

What a meeting it was! It was Christmas morning. The hall was packed. More than three thousand were in it. Hundreds were outside. Everything went wrong. Girl workers dressed in khaki were brought up from Georgetown and set on the platform. The Union Jack covered the table. A choir sang patriotic songs. Dozens of police were in the hall. Everything which the men regarded as 'kidding' was there.

As Mr. Lloyd George entered the choir started *See the Conquering Hero* comes. Then pandemonium broke loose. The audience started the *Red Flag*. . . . As Mr. Lloyd George sat down, a lock of hair strayed over his brow. Shouts of 'Get your hair cut! . . . came from all quarters. . . .

'Uncle Arthur' [Henderson] as chairman, spoke in his most paternal manner, and far too long. We were all keyed up about the Munitions Act, but Uncle Arthur spoke about the neutrality of Belgium and the origins of the war. He had a bad time. Mr. Lloyd George began badly. He looked unwell. Very tired. The meeting was pitiless. . . . I . . . called on them to give Mr. Lloyd George a hearing. They were quieter and, seizing the chance, Lloyd George showed them

Lloyd George in Glasgow, December 1915

what speaking could be like. He held them by describing quarrels about trade union conditions at such a time as haggling with an earthquake. . . . Then he rolled off burning sentences about love of country and . . . the row started again. The meeting ended as a fiasco.

This public rebuff for the Minister of Munitions—for with 3,000 tongues wagging it was soon no secret on Clydeside, even though a totally misleading account was released to the press—was to prove a costly victory for the Clyde Workers Committee. It was as though the government had come to a New Year Resolution to assert itself, for during the next four months it struck back with determination. By lunchtime on New Year's Day 1916 the troops were in at the offices of *Forward,* which had carried a truthful description of the famous meeting; the paper was suppressed and unsold copies impounded. The shop stewards restored by starting their own new paper, *The Worker,* financed by the expense allowances of 7s 6d given to everyone invited to St Andrew's Hall, but this lasted only four issues before also being shut down, on 2nd February. That day William Gallacher, and two other men closely associated with the papers were arrested under the Defence of the Realm Act, on charges of having published material calculated 'to cause mutiny, sedition or disaffection among the civilian population and to impede delay and restrict the production of war material'.

Meanwhile, on 5th January 1916, Mr Asquith had thrown down a new challenge to the anti-war faction by introducing the first conscription Bill in British history. The mere idea of compulsory military service struck deep at the most cherished beliefs of many people on the left, not merely the factory militants, and the I.L.P. and Clydeside Workers Committee jointly organised a large anti-conscription demonstration on Glasgow Green; but their stand gained little support. The local Trades Council rejected any suggestion of a general call for strike action and even in the most strike-prone factories it proved impossible to work up much protest; skilled munition workers were after all in little danger of being sent to the trenches.

The introduction of conscription strengthened the government's hand—if men could be compelled to join the Forces why should others not make sacrifices in their working lives?—and the danger of having one's exemption withdrawn probably played some part in damping down militancy. Early in January 1916 the Chief Constable of Glasgow enquired about obtaining military assistance if, as he foresaw, there was widespread trouble when forty men from the gun-mounting shop at Beardmore's shipbuilding and munition works at Dalmuir were prosecuted for striking in support of a shop steward who had been dismissed for swearing at the management. The men were found guilty and fined but not a man walked out in protest. (The authorities, leaving well alone, made, however, no effort to collect the offenders' fines.)

But the really explosive issue was dilution and on 21st January 1916 Asquith announced that this would go ahead. Only three days later, three Commissioners arrived from London to enforce dilution on the Clyde, being warmly welcomed by the Ministry of Munitions' Director for Scotland, William Weir, who had resigned as managing director of his own company in the previous Summer and was eager for a showdown with the militants. Already in October he had complained to Lloyd George's Parliamentary Secretary,

Christopher Addison (later Lord Addison) of 'the fallacy . . . that bargaining was necessary. . . . The men would have loyally done whatever the country required of them, if the position had been put to them' and he was ready, indeed eager, to see martial law imposed on the Clyde if milder methods failed.

By now the government was anxious to crush the Clyde Workers Committee. As early as November one Admiralty official had minuted bluntly: 'To obtain a reasonably smooth working of the Munitions Act this committee should be smashed' and, only a week later, even so liberal minded a man as William Beveridge (later Lord Beveridge), one of the chief draftsman of the Act, had advised that Gallacher and others who had signed the Committee's first leaflet should be prosecuted. The Ministry's permanent secretary, Sir Hubert Llewellyn Smith, who, as a very young Civil Servant had observed and chronicled the Great Dock Strike, advised that anyone inciting others to strike against dilution should be dealt with under D.O.R.A. and that 'police and military protection' should be given 'to all who are willing to work'.

Apart from the urgent need to introduce dilution the Ministry of Munitions hoped that this might provide the issue which would enable them to rid themselves of the Clydeside Workers Committee. Like Lloyd George before them the Ministry's Commissioners were perfectly prepared to deal with shop stewards in individual factories, but not with the committee as a body, and they knew well that the Committee's power rested on a few dominant individuals. 'I am afraid', warned the Ministry's Labour Officer for the area, on 17th January, 'that the removal of almost any one of these men . . . would at once cause a big strike'.

Undeterred the Commissioners went ahead and soon discovered that many shop stewards were delighted to find themselves consulted as equal partners with management, even on so sensitive a subject as dilution. But the real breakthrough came at one of the likeliest trouble-spots, Parkhead, where David Kirkwood, never wholly at one with his colleagues since he acknowledged that the war could not simply be ignored, accepted a scheme drafted by the 'moderate' John Wheatley, and for the third time,—as in the 'twopenny strike', and in the planned refusal to meet Lloyd George at Christmas—broke the militants' front. Essentially the scheme laid down that dilution would be the responsibility everywhere of a joint worker/management committee and that skilled men would not earn less because of it and might earn more, since the total cost of any operation would not be less than before, though part of it might now be performed by a less skilled employee. Outflanked for once the Clydeside Workers Committee hastily tried to make the policy their own and added new demands such as that any new entrant must join a union 'to be decided by the Shop Committee', but they discovered that soldiers' wives, who made up many of the new recruits, refused to be told by zealous shop stewards that it was their duty to their workmates to restrict their output and soon it was clear that the government had won. By August 1916 more than 10,000 dilutees, 90% of them women, had been introduced into engineering work in shipyards and munitions factories on the Clyde, enabling 7,400 skilled men to move to new jobs. In Weir's, where one of the hardest battles had been feared, by the end of the war the group's total labour force had doubled and

2,000 of the new workers were women, whose presence would have seemed inconceivable in 1914.

But the Clyde was not tamed without a battle. On 9th February, following the arrest of Gallacher, 10,000 workers had walked out, not merely from Gallacher's own works, but also from four other factories, though after the accused men had been given bail they rapidly went back. Two weeks later, on 26th February, trouble blew up at Parkhead, where Sir William Beardmore suddenly withdrew David Kirkwood's right as convener of shop stewards to wander freely about the works. The move may have been intended to provoke a confrontation, and if so it succeeded: on 17th March 1916 1,000 of Kirkwood's engineers went on strike, followed by a walk-out at several other plants which did work for Beardmore's, and later by others like Gallacher's Albion works, until by the end of the month 4,500 were out. But Gallacher, perhaps at first because of jealousy or dislike of Kirkwood and his position at Parkhead, mysteriously ruled 'out of order' an attempt to bring out all the factories on the Clyde represented on the Committee. The strike collapsed and a mass walk-out threatened if the government did not reduce food prices hardly got going. By March 30th the men who had struck in support of Kirkwood were already drifting back to work and when some of the ringleaders were prosecuted and fined, from £5 to £25, 'not a dog barked'.

Munition workers (notice the men's warning chalked on the board behind)

1916

MANIFESTO FROM PARKHEAD FORGE ENGINEERS
TO THEIR FELLOW WORKERS.

Fellow Workers,

We stopped work on Friday, 17th inst., and have been on strike since.

During the eighteen months of war our Shop Stewards have given every possible assistance towards increasing the output. The Convener, Bro. David Kirkwood, has been specially active in this respect, having, with the approval of the management, used all his influence in removing every cause of friction and even in finding the ever necessary additional labour. While labour was scarce and no chance of reducing our status existed, our employers granted facilities to Bro. Kirkwood to visit the various engineering departments where in the interest of the workers or the joint interest of workers and employers his service as Chief Shop Steward was temporarily required. The utmost harmony prevailed, and the management expressed gratification with such friendly relations.

About two months ago the Commissioners appointed by the Government to introduce the scheme for the dilution of labour to the Clyde area visited Parkhead. We received them in the most cordial manner, and an agreement was made by which the employers pledged themselves not to use this scheme for the purpose of introducing cheap labour and also to give a Committee appointed by the skilled workers an opportunity of seeing that this pledge was kept. But immediately after our consent to the scheme was obtained a new spirit was felt in the workshops. Soldiers, mostly Englishmen, were brought in, and these refused to join a trade union.

An agreement existed to the effect that all men employed must be trade unionists, but in the case of the soldiers the foreman did not apply this rule, as they did with other tradesmen engaged, and we had no means of enforcing compliance with it. In one shop, known as the 15-inch shell shop, over 100 men were put to work at lathes turning these shells and at horizontal boring machines boring these shells at a rate of sixpence per hour. Machines of this type have been always manned by tradesmen who received the standard rate of wages for engineers in the district. In another shop, known as the Howitzer shop, women were introduced, and on our Shop Stewards visiting this shop to ascertain the conditions of female labour the management strongly protested and contended that Bro. Kirkwood or any other Shop Steward had no right to discuss the question of wages or conditions with the women workers. Previously our Chief Shop Steward had perfect freedom to visit this shop if he felt it necessary to do so.

Next came instructions to our Chief Shop Steward, Bro. Kirkwood, that on no account was he to leave his bench without permission from the management during working hours. All these things and various smaller changes made it obvious to us that our trade union representatives were to be bound and blind-folded while the trade by which our means of life are obtained was being reduced in the interest of capitalists to the level of the most lowly occupation.

We feel that during the period when unskilled labour is engaged in our industry that more than ordinary freedom is required by our Shop Stewards to insure that under the cloak of patriotism greedy employers are not allowed to ruin our trade. This would be a very modest demand on our employers in view of the concessions we have made, but instead of being granted the greater facilities necessary we are being deprived, as already stated, of the limited freedom we enjoyed.

In reply to the question as to why we did not act through official channels we wish to state that we submitted our grievance about the introduction of non-union soldiers to the Board of Trade, but, so far as we know, our complaint was not noticed. We directed the attention of our paid officials to the cheap labour in the shell shop, but they have failed to protect us. Therefore, when the restriction was imposed on our Shop Stewards we felt that our only hope lay in drastic action by ourselves.

Fellow-workers, we are fighting the battle of all workers. If they smash us they will smash you. Our victory will be your victory. Unite with us in demanding that during the present crisis our Shop Stewards in every workshop where dilution is in force shall have the fullest liberty to investigate the conditions under which the new class labour is employed, so that this may not be used to reduce us all to a lower standard of life.

The strike at Parkhead

David Kirkwood was not there to see his faithful followers defeated. At 3 o'clock in the morning of Saturday 25th March 1916, soon after the strike at Parkhead had begun, he was arrested by four armed detectives on a warrant under the Defence of the Realm Act and 'deported' to Edinburgh, along with five other leading militants, among them James Messer of Weir's and Gallacher's ally Arthur MacManus. The 'deportees' were well treated and allowed to go anywhere they wished, except Glasgow. The others took work in England, but Kirkwood himself, when the order was revoked a year later, returned to his old firm. By now the government's counter-attack on the Clydeside Workers Committee was well under way. On 14th April, while a batch of strikers were being fined in Glasgow, William Gallacher and his two fellow accused, on bail since February, came up for trial in Edinburgh. Gallacher was sent to prison for a year, while his fellow accused received 12 months and three months respectively. Their case was hardly helped by an air raid on Edinburgh the night before nor by John Maclean, who was tried shortly before them on other charges of sedition and delivered an impassioned speech from the dock in which he declared that 'I stand here not as the accused, but as the accuser of capitalism dripping with blood from head to foot'. But capitalism, if bloody, was unbowed. Maclean got three years in jail.

A week after Gallacher's trial James Maxton and two other anti-war campaigners also received sentences of from twelve to eighteen months, so that all told seven Clydeside militants were sent to prison for sedition and six compulsorily removed from the area.

This modest exercise of force proved sufficient to break the hold of the Committee on the Clyde. 'The movement', recorded Gallacher with disgust, 'fell into the hands of some S.L.P. [Socialist Labour Party] sectarians, who stifled all possible expression of a fighting character. . . . They were for "educating" the workers. But no fight against the war, no strikes'.

For Red Clydeside it was a sad comedown. And it was an even sadder one when on 29th June 1917 Lloyd George returned to Glasgow to be given the freedom of the city, though the militants took what consolation they could from the fact that he needed a strong police guard, and from the release next day, with half his sentence still unserved, of John Maclean. But within a few months, Maclean—one of nature's martyrs—had succeeded in talking himself back into jail again, this time for five years. He was released prematurely once more at the end of the war, in time to stand in the 'coupon' election of 1918 against an alleged 'traitor to the working class', a former Labour M.P. and coalition minister, George Barnes. Maclean, despite the Lloyd George landslide, collected a respectable 7,400 votes against his opponent's 14,200, fighting on a straight 'revolutionary' ticket, a reminder that the spirit of the Clyde Workers Committee was not dead yet.

Nor was the legend of the Red Clyde. What seemed likely to be the most serious disturbance of all occurred as the immediate post-war slump hit Glasgow with the inevitable sharp falling off in the orders for ships and munitions, so that unemployment, which had been insignificant in both engineering and shipbuilding during the war (0.5% and 0.15% respectively) soared suddenly so that by February 1919, it had reached 11% and 4%, even before demobilisation had begun and wartime contracts had run out. The revived Clydeside Workers Committee, dominated once again by Gallacher and Messer, were soon demanding a general strike in the West of Scotland to support a visionary programme to curb unemployment, including a thirty hour week. Others had different programmes. The Trades Council, presided over by Shinwell, was prepared to campaign for a forty hour week. The Associated Society of Engineers, was willing to settle for forty seven hours. Eventually most factories and shipyards agreed to come out, and what Shinwell called 'the greatest strike that has ever taken place in the industrial world' began in earnest on 27th January. Within a few days 100,000 people, a high proportion of the total work force, were out in Glasgow alone—including it need hardly be said, the workers at such familiar battlegrounds as Parkhead Forge

and Weir's. More serious to the population as a whole, the city was without gas or electricity and the movement was beginning to spread to Edinburgh and Leith.

The government, with the spectacle of the Russian revolution before them, reacted a little as Pitt and Perceval had done at the time of the Napoleonic wars. This, they suspected, might be the start of the long-feared Bolshevik revolution, or at least of the almost equally dreaded General Strike, and some of the wilder spirits had indeed already prepared plans to sabotage the electricity supply. Then, on the morning of Friday 31st January, the expected violence occurred. Shinwell, Gallacher and Kirkwood, having asked the Lord Provost to plead with the government to grant their demands, especially the forty hour week, called at the City Chambers to receive its

The Red Flag in George Square, Glasgow

A demonstration of military force, February 1919

Tanks at the Meat Market, Glasgow, February 1919

The strike leaders on trial (Left to right: Emmanuel Shinwell, George Ebury, David Brennan, David Kirkwood, Harry Hopkins and James Murray)

answer—it was, of course, a refusal—with at their back, like Ben Tillett at the start of the Dock Strike, an army of unemployed and strikers. When the police tried to clear a way for a tram through the demonstrators packed into St George's Square outside, violent fighting broke out. A full scale clash with the mounted police followed, the Riot Act was read, and after the square had been cleared, an angry crowd rampaged through the city. Although this was soon labelled 'Bloody Friday' no-one was killed though both Gallacher and Kirkwood were injured, but by morning the City Chambers were surrounded by barbed wire and protected by machine guns, while garrisons of troops were stationed in other public buildings, patrols of armed soldiers marched about the streets and—most impressive of all—six huge tanks, a weapon never before used in civil disturbances in Britain, waited in the Meat Market to subdue the rebellious citizens.

Once again, the strong line paid off. On the 12th February, with men drifting back to work, the committee in charge called the strike off and in April the ringleaders, apart from Kirkwood, who was acquitted, were sent to jail, Gallacher and two others for three months, Shinwell for five.

The leaders of Red Clydeside split soon afterwards. Two years later Gallacher and most of the surviving leaders of the Clyde Workers Committee found their true home, with the founding of the Communist Party of Great Britain. Kirkwood, Shinwell, Maxton and all but the most extreme of the I.L.P. now turned firmly and finally to democratic and constitutional methods, with immediate results. In 1922 the I.L.P. won ten out of fifteen Glasgow seats in the General Election and almost every famous I.L.P. name became an M.P. simultaneously, including Kirkwood, Shinwell, Maxton and Wheatley. But the reconciliation with the 'establishment' and the politics of peaceful persuasion was not yet complete. As they travelled south to Westminster the Clydesiders, as they were soon known in the House, discovered the eminent Labour lawyer, Sir Patrick Hastings was on the same train and went to him with an urgent and important enquiry: If a member were suspended for causing a disturbance in the House did he still receive his salary?

5 Collective bargaining freely conducted

The provisions of this Act shall have effect for the purpose of promoting good industrial relations in accordance with. . . . The principle of collective bargaining freely conducted . . . with due regard to the general interests of the community. . . . The principle of free association of workers in independent trade unions.
Preamble to the Industrial Relations Act 1971.

The Great War raised the status of the working class in the community. Rich and poor alike had, whether as volunteers or conscripts, fought alongside each other and it had for the first time been recognized that the men at the front were dependent upon the miners, railwaymen and munition workers at home. The malcontents of the Clyde and similar areas apart, the war also seemed at first to have generated an unprecedented feeling of unity; the 'two nations' joined in a common purpose, had for a time become one. But, once the euphoria of victory had evaporated, and disillusionment at the squandering of life in Flanders spread, it became clear that the gulf was as wide as ever. The most basic division of all, between those whose income was relatively secure and those who lived only from week to week, far from being diminished was soon sharper than ever. Between 1850 and 1914 the proportion of trade union members out of work—the only section of the working population for whom such statistics were then available— oscillated between 1 or 2 and 10 or 12%,

according to the state of trade. Between 1921 and 1937 unemployment among trade unionists averaged 14%; the former short-term maximum had now become the irreducible, apparently permanent minimum. In the worst year of all, 1932, 22.8% of the whole insured population— including those who did not belong to a union—were 'on the dole', more than one worker in every five.

This grim figure, however, masked even greater human tragedies, for unemployment varied enormously between different parts of the country, and it was the areas whose prosperity depended on Britain's traditional industries which suffered worst as their overseas markets dried up or as the countries concerned developed their own native industries. Textiles were the classic case, and India the classic example of this process, its needs for cloth soon being met largely from its own resources.

Exports of manufactured cotton goods were by 1924 only two thirds of what they had been in 1912, by 1930 well below a half, by 1935 much less than a third. The export of woollen and worsted 'tissues' also dropped markedly, being by 1930 little more than half the pre-war amount. Equally striking was the declining demand for coal. In the four years before the war the British Isles had produced 25% of all the world's coal; by 1937 their share was down to 19%. In 1913 287 million tons had been mined, of which 73 million had been sold abroad. The comparable figures for 1932 were 209 million tons produced, of which only 39 million were exported. Here was the fundamental explanation for the miners with their fading war medals playing mouth organs on street corners, which so vividly symbolise those bitter years. In 1913 the mines had provided work for 1,105,000 men; by 1932 they needed only 819,000. The other basic industries—shipbuilding, agriculture, heavy engineering,—suffered similarly. The unemployment map of Great Britain reflected the simple facts of economic geography. London, the South East and the South-West, the homes of the 'new industries'—chemicals, radio and electrical goods, the expanding 'service' trades—got off comparatively lightly with, even in the

depth of the depression in July 1932, only from 13.1–16.4% of the adult insured population out of work. In the engineering-centred Midlands the figure rose to 21%; in the heavy industry and textile belt of the North West and North East to 26.3–30%; in Scotland, with its mines and shipbuilding, to 29%; in Wales—where the misery of the mining valleys became a legend—to 38.1%, the worst, and saddest, such statistic of the century. Over the whole United Kingdom 2,843,000 men and women—plus others not covered by National Insurance—were out of work in 1932. Not till 1936 did unemployment fall below the two million mark and not till 1940 below one million.

The shock of mass unemployment was all the greater because like the notorious 'hard-

YESTERDAY-THE TRENCHES

TO-DAY-UNEMPLOYED

faced men' of the post-war House of
Commons, many manual workers, exploiting
to the full their scarcity value at a time of
national crisis had also 'done well out of the
war'. The munition workers on the Clyde
and elsewhere who had, whether for
honourable reasons or not, escaped the call-
up and stayed at home to earn high wages
in safety instead of rotting on a private's
pittance in France, now discovered with
shocked surprise that they could not also
escape the post-war slump.

The trade unions had also gained from
the war, in membership, which rose from
4,145,000 in 1914 to 6,533,000 in 1918,
and in their standing in the community; the
government had carefully cultivated them
as allies and had, in 1916, created a special
Ministry of Labour to deal with the very
matters that concerned them most, an
innovation which continued after the war.
But, given the trade unions' awareness of
their power, the worsening economic
climate, and the habit which had grown up
of 'blaming the boss' for any inconvenient
fact of economic life, a collision between
government and workers was perhaps
inevitable. The clash came, predictably, in
the mines, which during the war had been
virtually run by the state but were now,
against the wishes of the Miners
Federation, handed back to private
management. The Federation also called for
higher wages and a six hour working day;
the mine-owners retorted that, on the
contrary the mines could only survive at all
if the industry cut its costs and become
more competitive, which meant essentially

Two aspects of poverty.

*Miner's wife entering a pawnshop during a strike in
the 1920's.*

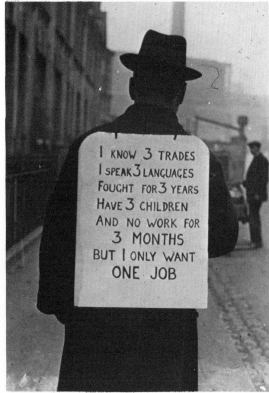

Unemployed man in the 1930's.

more work for less money.

While the situation, not merely in the mines but in British industry generally, was deteriorating, the first Labour government took power, in 1924. According to the historian of the Trade Union Congress the new ministers 'more or less consistently cold-shouldered the T.U.C. and its leaders' and it seemed to many trade unionists that Ramsay Macdonald was more anxious to establish his government's respectability (as indeed he was, with an eye to Labour's long-term prospects) than to serve the immediate purposes of organised labour, much less wage the class war. The circumstances of the government's fall, over the Campbell case, (when it unwisely dropped a prosecution for sedition against a mutilated ex-serviceman which it had even more unwisely started) and its subsequent rout at the polls, due to the unscrupulous 'Red letter' stunt, did nothing to increase confidence among the 'wild men' of the Left in constitutional and parliamentary methods.[1] The new Conservative government, however, was even less to the T.U.C.'s liking, since, its historian considers, it 'saw no reason not to continue' the 'conveniently cool policy' followed by its predecessor and preferably

[1] 'Red Clydeside' cast its shadow over both events: J. R. Campbell had been a close associate of James Maxton, while the Zinoviev letter was addressed to a former Clydesider, now President of the newly-founded Communist Party of Great Britain, Arthur MacManus, one of those deported from Glasgow in 1916.

The leaders of the first Labour Government leaving Buckingham Palace, January 1924. From left to right: Ramsay Macdonald, 'Jimmy' Thomas and Arthur Henderson.

to improve on it'. Even worse the new Chancellor, Winston Churchill, insisted on a return to the Gold Standard, 'a move which inevitably played havoc with British exports', while the Prime Minister Stanley Baldwin warned that, in order to keep prices competitive, 'all workers in this country have got to take reductions in wages'. The first victims of this policy were the miners, who, beside a cut in rates of pay, were asked to return, from their current seven hour shifts, to an eight hour day. Their response was contained in the famous slogan 'Not a penny off the pay not a second on the day' and an appeal for help to the T.U.C., and especially their old allies the railwaymen and the transport workers. ... duly promised, that, if it came to a

strike, they would not move a single wagon load of coal from the vast stocks already above ground. 'We have made arrangements', the miners' tough and truculent leader Arthur Cook warned the prime minister, 'that not one ton of coal will be handled in this country unless the government's decision is satisfactory to us miners. We are going to be slaves no longer and our men will starve before they accept any reduction of wages.' This was fighting talk, but not unfamiliar in such situations. What was new, was that the General Council of the Trades Union Congress, rather to its own surprise, found itself promising all-out support for the miners with what it liked to describe as a National Strike. Cook also issued a direct challenge to Parliament:

Let me warn the government that there is a new mentality in the police, the army, the navy and the air force. Ninety-seven per cent of the recruits for the past two years have come from the working classes and thousands of them [are former] miners, who will not shoot against their kith and kin when the order comes. . . . This is a war to the death.

No Cabinet, not even that headed by the honourable and peaceable Stanley Baldwin could ignore such language, even though he was certainly in earnest when he told the T.U.C. Negotiating Committee on 29th April, 'We have striven, we have pleaded, we have begged for peace. . . . The nation wants peace. Those who want war must take the responsibility'. Privately he warned the Labour leader, 'Jimmy' Thomas, that if a General strike did occur he might find himself forced to take strong measures

committee arrested' and, worst of all, 'greater play', meaning 'pickets killed'. Only the Miners Federation, with nothing to lose, were resigned to, or eager for, a show-down.

The government's final attempt to avert disaster was to set up the Samuel Commission, which produced a Report considered by Lord Samuel himself 'very favourable to the miners'. It offered a variety of benefits including pit-head baths and, ultimately, holidays with pay, but warned that only lower wages or lower hours could avert 'the disaster impending over the industry' and that the existing government subsidy must be allowed to expire. Cook and his colleagues, however, dismissed the

The miners' champion. Arthur Cook in full voice in Trafalgar Square.

Report as 'a declaration of war against the miners and the whole working class movement'; the stage was set for a head-on clash.

On Friday 30th April the government subsidy to the mines expired and the mine-owners' final offer, which involved a 13% reduction in pay and a return to the eight hour day, was rejected. The miners, having refused to return to work on these terms, were locked out. A General Strike might still have been avoided, but, in the early hours of Monday 3rd May 1926, the compositors on the *Daily Mail* refused to set an anti-union article and the government interpreted this as the opening of hostilities. The T.U.C. had little option but to call its members out and next morning the General Strike began. The million miners on strike were rapidly joined by one and half million railwaymen, transport workers, printers, builders and iron and steel workers, followed, several days later, by engineers and shipyard workers and by others who came out in sympathy. But many industries were not affected at all, including the Post Office and the distributive trades, and, apart from those on strike, it was only the absence of transport and newspapers which really affected daily life.

If the government took comfort from this, and from the rush of volunteers into the Organisation for the Maintenance of Supplies, which worked smoothly, the T.U.C.

Condensed milk awaiting distribution during the General Strike was encouraged by the response among those actually called out. On 4th May, only one driver or guard in every hundred turned up for work, and the docks and roads were equally silent. Despite the efforts of amateur 'blacklegs', only 40 of 4,400 London buses were back on the road by the end of the week, and of 2,000 trams only nine, though in a few provincial cities public transport was hardly disrupted at all. Although the manual workers in most power stations walked out, supplies of electricity were kept going by engineers and outside helpers, perhaps to the relief of the T.U.C., who ordered local strike committees to provide electricity for 'such services as house, street and shop lighting, social services . . . bakeries, laundries and domestic purposes', a long list which left few non-industrial premises unserved. The strike-leaders also refused to interfere with the distribution of milk, food and medicines and permits for the transport of essential goods were issued on a generous scale. All this did more credit to the T.U.C.'s humanity than to their generalship; it might be magnificent but it was certainly not all-out war.

The truth was that, despite the steadily gathering volume of support for it from among trade unionists, their leaders were from the first half-hearted about the General Strike. A declaration by a former Attorney General, Sir John Simon, that they were

Rallying round. Society ladies cooking for voluntary workers at the food distribution centre in Hyde Park.

acting illegally and liable to prosecution for conspiracy and the payment of fringe damages, though almost certainly wrong in law, encouraged their loss of nerve.

The refusal of the miners' leaders, on Wednesday 12th May, to accept a new government compromise—though it offered virtually the same terms as before—gave the T.U.C. the excuse it needed. The strike was called off: It had been literally a nine days' wonder. 'A spirit of fatalism came over the workers', wrote one observer in Manchester. 'The T.U.C. had ordered them back; there was no hope of concerted resistance—so back they went'—when they were allowed to, for the government had warned that it could not guarantee that the employers would reinstate all those who had walked out. Some unions, in some places, stayed out for a few days more, to try and prevent such victimisation, as they called it, but only the miners fought on for long, work not being generally resumed until the end of November, after a lock-out lasting seven months. They then returned on the terms they had previously requested. The General Strike, the most serious threat to an elected government in British history, had ended in complete surrender by the trades unions.

'Before myself and my colleagues', wrote the young Walter Citrine, the T.U.C.'s recently-appointed General Secretary, 'an abyss had opened. It was the culmination of days and days of faint heartedness'.

Keeping up morale. A meeting in support of the strikers on Peckham Rye.

Keeping the power going. Servicemen unloading supplies at Neasden Power Station.

Maintaining food supplies. Armoured cars protecting a supply convoy in East India Dock Road.

George Lansbury, a future leader of the Labour Party, strove to hit a more cheerful note, in *Lansbury's Bulletin,* circulated in Poplar, where a generation before the dockers' epic struggle had ended in total victory. 'We have had our General Strike. Imperfect as it has been . . . it has been the most magnificent effort of rank-and-file solidarity that the British movement has ever displayed.'

Perhaps the most apposite summing up of all came from Beatrice Webb, now the grand old lady of the Labour Party and written the day before the strike started:

The net impression left on my mind is that the General Strike will turn out not to be a revolution of any sort but a batch of compulsory Bank

Holidays. . . . When the million or so strikers have spent their money they will drift back to work and no one will be any better off and many will be a great deal poorer and everybody will be cross.

The first consequence of defeat for the unions was the passing of the Trade Disputes and Trades Union Act, which expressly made illegal any future attempt to 'coerce the government either directly or by inflicting hardship on the community', banned sympathetic strikes in an industry not directly involved in a dispute, and forbad Civil Servants to belong to any union affiliated to the T.U.C. To the great indignation of the Labour Party it also substituted 'contracting in' for 'contracting out' in the payment of the political levy to

All over. Special constables going off duty at the end of the Strike.

trade unions, severely reducing its income.*

The Party's finances, like those of the unions themselves, also suffered from the other major result of the General Strike, a sharp decline in union membership which from 6,533,000 in 1918 had risen by 1920 to 8,348,000, only to fall off sharply as the effects of the depression began to be felt. By 1922, in a working population of about 19 and a half million, trade union membership was already down to 5,625,000 and by 1926 it had slumped still further to 4,366,000. The failure of the Strike accelerated this

trend, so that by 1928 membership was below 4 million and in 1934 it reached rock-bottom, for the inter-war period, of 3,295,000. Then a steady recovery began, until the four million figure was regained in 1937, five million being reached in 1941 and 6 million in 1943. In addition to these totals there were other organised workers, like Civil Servants, in unions not affiliated to the T.U.C. Even excluding these organisations membership during the interwar period came to spread over a far larger number of occupations than before, for the former backbone of the movement, the miners and textile workers, who in 1914 had accounted for over 30% of total union

---

* The Trade Disputes Act was later repealed by the Labour Government elected in 1945.

One contemporary view of the strike.

Two men against the strike.
Stanley Baldwin, Prime Minister in 1926.

Winston Churchill, who edited the government
newspaper 'The British Gazette'.

Two trade unionists. Ernest Bevin, of the Transport
and General Workers Union, later Minister of Labour.

Walter (later Lord) Citrine, General Secretary of the
Trades Union Congress in 1926.

membership formed, by 1927, little more than a fifth. Much of the growth had occurred in the transport industries and among unskilled workers, and the relative power of both these groups, as of many others, had been strengthened by the wholesale amalgamation of smaller unions which was a feature of this period. Two of the 'Big Six' unions had already been formed, the Miners Federation of Great Britain (later renamed the National Union of Mineworkers), in 1889 and the National Union of Railwaymen, in 1913, but the four others were created in mergers during the 1920s. John Burns's old union, and the centre of the Clydeside troubles, the Amalgamated Society of Engineers, became in 1920, the Amalgamated Engineering Union; Will Thorne's National Union of Gasworkers and General Labourers, dating from 1889, and various others, combined to form the National Union of General and Municipal Workers in 1924; a number of unions covering Co-operative employees and others coalesced in 1921 into the Union of Shop, Distributive and Allied Workers; and under the dynamic direction of Ernest Bevin, fourteen separate unions

September 1931. Schoolteachers demonstrate against a 15% cut in their salaries, part of the National Government's economy programme.

were cajoled and bludgeoned in 1922 into forming the enormous Transport and General Workers Union, which absorbed among other bodies the Dock Labourers Union founded by Ben Tillett during the Great Dock Strike. One of the 'Big Six', it will be noted, involved an extension of trade unionism from the workshop floor into the distributive trades, and two other new unions formed at this time also revealed a marked widening of the base of the trade union movement, the Union of Post Office Workers, created in 1920, which was immediately successful, attracting 100,000 recruits from a potential 190,000, and the Civil Service Clerical Association, launched in 1922, a pio

overtime, but the difference an eight hour day (commonly followed by a half day on a Saturday) could make to a man's daily life was vividly described by a then G.W.R. fireman at Neyland in South Wales, one of the hundreds of thousands who gained when, in 1919, railwaymen's hours were cut from 60 to 48:

The two twelve-hour shifts had to be replaced with three eight-hour shifts and we had leisure time which we hadn't experienced since leaving school. . . . Part of every day took on the flavour of a holiday. The early morning shift of 6 a.m. until 2 p.m. seemed so short that we joked that it was hardly worth going in for. The afternoon shift of 2 p.m. until 10 p.m. seemed like a half-day with an extra bonus of lying in bed until

d the night shift of
morning seemed so
ooked on than
. No longer were
uring the day.
ldren populated
men either at
nd middle-aged
nd gossipers,
zed with all
acquired.

practised,
, farmers
ing rights
ymaking,
rospered,
er rarely
. More

lug.

ore
ore

o

professions and among clerical staff, but as late as 1925 only about one and a half million wage earners received paid holidays, and by April 1937 no more than one and three quarter million. The transformation came in 1938 with legislation in theory enabling, in practice requiring, certain industries, including agriculture, to grant paid holidays, and at the same time the Ministry of Labour began a drive to include such provisions in all agreements between workmen and employers in which it was involved. By November 1938 the total covered by such agreement, had already risen to nine million and by June 1939 to 11 million, in a total 'working class' (drawing the line, as was then customary, at the £5 a week level) of around 18 and a half million. At this time the normal allowance consisted of one week plus public holidays, though 'advanced' employers like the public utilities and the Civil Service already provided two weeks or more, and this trend has continued until today a minimum of two weeks, plus Bank Holidays and occasionally extra days linked to them, is universal, and up to four weeks, even for manual workers, is becoming increasingly common.

For most of those who profited by it their first holiday with pay was also the last they enjoyed in peace time and from September 1939 to August 1945 the trade unions were, like everyone else, preoccupied with winning the war. In May 1940 the already legendary

'I appeal'. A woman appears before an Appeal Board to appeal against an order directing her to a particular war job during World War II. (The panel consists of a chairman appointed by the Ministry of Labour, an employers' representative, and an employees' representative nominated by a trade union.)

Ernest Bevin, of the Transport and General Workers Union, became Minister of Labour, a post he filled with conspicuous success. Bevin involved the trade unions in the war effort with the minimum of dispute or even argument, though there were a few strikes—including one in the mines which led to many of the strikers being prosecuted—and occasional demands, sometimes granted for the sake of peace, for craftsmen's privileges to be protected.

The importation, by volunteering or by direction, of millions of workers into new jobs, and the recruitment for war work of vast numbers of women, from young girls to victims of the 'grannies call up' aged up to fifty-one, was accomplished with remarkably little trouble or even rancour.

After the war the trend towards social equality continued, encouraged by the Labour government's far-ranging legislative programme. This not merely provided for the working class family many traditional middle-class benefits, such as increased educational opportunities, but it also extended (as is often forgotten) to the middle-class, advantages previously confined to those below a certain income, such as state insurance against sickness. As a means of reducing class barriers such measures were far more significant than the nationalisation between 1947 and 1951 of the mines, railways and other essential industries which, as was soon being pointed out, often made little immediate or obvious difference either to their employees or to their customers.

The outstanding feature of the industrial scene in the past thirty years has undoubtedly been the absence of mass unemployment on a pre-war scale, and especially of the long-term unemployment that left men to lose their skills, health and spirits as one idle year followed another. Between 1946 and 1960 the highest level of unemployment reached—490,000 in 1952—would have seemed unbelievably small by pre-war standards, and for most of those fifteen years the total was no higher than 200,000 or 300,000, the lowest figure 215,000, being reached in 1951. From 1960 to 1974 the trend was slightly but not alarmingly upwards, and apart from brief periods of short-time working due to strikes or power cuts, the number unemployed has ranged between 347,000 (in 1965) and 885,500 in 1972. The average in 1973 was 598,000 in a working population of 25,490,000, and in 1974 around 580,000. Though serious enough for those concerned, to be unemployed now is a very different matter from being out of work in the 1930s, and the benefits available to any family in distress are incomparably better. For practical purposes the permanent insecurity and danger of real hunger which have underlain working class life ever since the Industrial Revolution have now disappeared even if not all the feelings and attitudes which they generated have done so.

It is no doubt the realisation that governments and employers both tend to be on the side of the big battalions that has led to one of the two most significant developments in trade union history since the war, the growth of the white-collar unions, especially in areas, such as banking and among hospital staff, where before the war union membership (except perhaps of some employer inspired 'Staff Association') would have seemed unthinkable. Of the 109 unions represented at the Trades Union Congress in 1973, no fewer than 65 contained some non-manual members, though the vast majority of white-collar trade unionists were concentrated in a few organisations like the

'Equal pay now!' Militant women on the march.

'Fair pay for Civil Servants!' A white-collar worker demonstrates against a 'freeze' of Civil Servants pay, January 1973.

National Association of Local Government Officers and the Civil Service unions. In a total membership of unions affiliated to the T.U.C. (those outside are numerically unimportant) of 10,022,224, non-manual employees amounted to 2,951,700, or approaching 30%, a proportion which seems likely to increase as automation increasingly upgrades jobs from 'manual' to 'white collar' and teachers, clerks, and executives of all kinds seek the protection of collective bargaining against a further erosion of their standard of living.

The other notable development in union membership since the war has been the rise in the number of women members, another group among whom in the past recruitment had been very limited. By 1973 they amounted to 2,603,016 of the 10 million

mentioned above, a formidable, and also growing, army. The real power of the trade union movement rests, however, as it always has done, with a few very large unions, for during the 1960s the process of amalgamation which had begun between the wars continued, with the shipbuilders, for example, becoming linked with the boilermakers and blacksmiths in 1963, and the Amalgamated Engineering Union embracing the Foundry Workers in 1968, so that already something like three quarters of all trade unionists belong to about twenty large organisations, able—as has been seen more than once in recent years— to bargain from positions of strength not merely with employers but governments.

The cry that 'the unions are getting too powerful' is one that has regularly been raised from the late eighteenth century onwards, and in recent years attempts have been made by both major parties to restrict their powers and freedom by new laws. Both have ended in failure. In January 1969, following the publication of the Donovan Report on industrial relations, six months earlier, the Labour government issued a White Paper *In Place of Strife* containing various proposals designed to discourage unofficial or casually-undertaken strikes. The government, it was proposed, should have power to order a 28 day 'conciliation' pause in a dispute, to order a strike ballot where necessary, and to intervene and impose a settlement in an inter-union dispute. Undoubtedly the plan received much public support but when the

government attempted to incorporate these principles in an Industrial Relations Bill it encountered such opposition from among its own supporters, as well as from the T.U.C., that early in 1970 it was dropped, a decision described by the most recent historian of British Trade Unionism as 'a major defeat for the government'. The Conservative Opposition naturally made the most of this rebuff, but after taking office themselves, in June 1970, proved little more successful in producing an enduring reform of the law. The Industrial Relations Act which finally passed into law on 5th August 1971, after protracted discussion in the Commons and a number of one-day protest strikes, was based on the general principle, according to the explanatory Guide issued

IN PLACE OF STRIFE

A POLICY FOR INDUSTRIAL RELATIONS

Presented to Parliament by the First Secretary of State and
Secretary of State for Employment and Productivity
by Command of Her Majesty
January 1969

The Labour White Paper of 1969.

Crown copyright.

RTY

soon afterwards, of 'freely conducted collective bargaining which pays due regard to the community's general interests' and the establishment of 'orderly procedures for settling disputes peacefully and speedily by negotiation, conciliation or arbitration'. The 'free association of workers in independent trade unions' and 'freedom and security for workers, protected by safeguards against unfair industrial practice' were also to be guaranteed. The Act was bitterly opposed by the unions and, though registering under it would have given them considerable advantages (such as protection for their funds and, in some cases, the right to impose a closed shop) the vast majority took the T.U.C.'s advice to boycott all the machinery connected with it and some even refused to recognise the authority of the Industrial Relations Court set up under the Act. The Court's prestige never recovered from a humiliating episode when, having committed three dockers to prison for contempt of court for defying its order to stop illegal picketing of some premises they had 'blacked', it had to stand idly by when, only five days later, their release was ordered by the Official Solicitor. Following the men's release the T.U.C. abandoned plans for a one day General Strike which it had called in protest against their imprisonment. When, however, in February 1974, the government, faced by a miners' strike as a result of its pay restraint policy, called a General Election, it failed to gain the support it had expected and the

The Prime Ministers and the unions. Harold Wilson tried, and failed, to introduce legislation in 1969 to control industrial relations. The attempt was abandoned in the face of opposition from the unions and from some members of his party. Edward Heath tried, and succeeded, in carrying an Industrial Relations Act, but it did not remain in force for long. Following a miners' strike and the subsequent general election he lost office to a Labour

'Portals of power'. T.U.C: headquarters, Congress House, opened in 1958.

At the T.U.C. Training College. At this course for union officers the T.U.C.'s Medical Adviser is discussing health hazards.

White-collar picket line. These three bank employees were handing out leaflets to customers during a strike demanding recognition of their union, November 1967.

CHAPTER _E_

The standard work is E. P. Thompson, *The Making of the English Working Class* (Penguin, 1968) which provided the information about William Lovett and about Friendly Society membership. Also very useful is G. D. H. Cole and Raymond Postgate, *The Common People* (Methuen, 1971) which quotes the breakdown of national wealth, prepared by Patrick Colquhoun. Francis Williams, *Magnificent Journey* (Odhams, 1954) though essentially journalistic, includes much useful material, including the 'loving shopmaites' letter and examples of trade union activity during the Combination Acts era. The passages quoted from William Cobbett all appear in the *Political Register* for the dates indicated (i.e. 7th December 1833; 5th April 1817 and 14th April 1821) and can be found in G. D. H. and Margaret Cole, *The Opinions of William Cobbett* (1944). Guy Boas (editor), *Selections from Cobbett's Rural Rides* (Macmillan, 1926) is also useful. The information about population and the breakdown of those engaged in 'trade, manufacture and handicraft' can be found in the *Census Reports, 1801–1841,* and particularly in John Rickman, *Comparative Account of the Population of Great Britain 1801–1831* (Parliamentary Accounts and Papers, Vol. XVIII, 1832). Edwin Chadwick, *The Sanitary Condition of the Labouring Population* (1842) is invaluable on living conditions a little later in the century. My major contemporary source, including information on wages, living conditions, factory conditions, public houses in Manchester, the 'proper weekly expenditure' of a prosperous weaver and the effect of machinery on the labourer's life was Peter Gaskell, *Machinery and Artisans, The Moral and Physical Condition of the Manufacturing Population Considered with Reference to Mechanical Substitutes for Human Labour,* (1836) which was first published as *The Manufacturing Population of England* (1832). Other details of earnings come from: G. D. H. Cole, *A Short History of the British Working Class Movement* (Allen and Unwin, 1966); Frances Collier, *The Family Economy of the Working Classes in the Cotton Industry 1784–1833* (Manchester

University Press, 1965); and G. R. Porter, *The Progress of the Nation in its Various Social and Economical Relations from the Beginning of the Nineteenth Century* (new edition, 1847). Samuel Bamford's life is described in his *Autobiography*, edited by W. H. Chaloner (two volumes, 1867). I used mainly the volume I, *Early Days* (first published 1848). The account of working hours at Tyldesley and the list of factory fines can be found in J. L. and Barbara Hammond, *The Town Labourer* (Longmans, 1919, reprinted Cedric Chivers, 1965). Other books I used included: Robert Owen, *Observations on the Effect of the Manufacturing System* (1818); C. P. Moritz, *Journeys of a German in England in 1782* (Cape, 1965); Elie Halevy, *A History of the English People in 1815* (Volume II, Economic Life) (Penguin, 1937); A. L. Morton, *A People's History of England* (Gollancz, 1938); E. Royston Pike (editor), *Human Documents of the Industrial Revolution* (Allen and Unwin, 1966); Elizabeth Burton, *The Georgians at Home* (Arrow Books, 1973); and Theo Barker (editor), *The Long March of Everyman* (Deutsch, 1975).

CHAPTER TWO

The chapter epigraph is quoted in Thompson and other information on the Luddites can be found in the Hammonds, *The Skilled Labourer,* Theo Barker, Halevy, who mentions the saying that 'Ned Ludd had passed this way', Cole and Postgate, who refer to 'King Ludd' and E. J. Hobsbawm, *Labouring Men* (Weidenfeld and Nicolson, 1964). The indispensable source is Frank Peel, *The Risings of the Luddites* (1888, reprinted Frank Cass, 1968) which has a useful introduction by E. P. Thompson, and other recent studies are Malcolm I. Thomis (editor), *Luddism in Nottinghamshire* (Thoroton Society, Phillimore, Chichester, 1967) and the same writer's *The Luddites, Machine-Breaking in Regency England* (David and Charles, 1970). The Luddite novel referred to, which includes the description of an initiation ceremony is D. F. E. Sykes and G. H. Walker, *Ben o' Bills, The Luddite, A Yorkshire Tale* (1898). Contemporary reports were drawn from *The Examiner*, 20 September 1812; The *Leeds Mercury*, 23 November 1811, 28 November 1811, 7 December 1811, 21 December 1811, 28 December 1811, 22 February 1812, 29 February 1812, 18 April 1812, 9 May 1812, 23 May 1812, 25 July 1812 and 22 August 1812; and the *Gentleman's Magazine*, January 1812, March 1812, April 1812 and September 1812. The report on the House of Lords debate, including Byron's speech, is in *Hansard* for 27 February 1812 and I also consulted the debate in the House of Commons on 17 February 1812.

CHAPTER THREE

The best and most recent account, on which I drew heavily, is Ann Stafford *A Match to Light the Thames* (Hodder and Stoughton, 1961). The two contemporary sources, from which I have also quoted extensively, are Henry Hyde Champion, *The Great Dock Strike, 1889* (1890), and Sir Hubert Llewellyn Smith and Vaughan Nash, *The Story of the Dockers' Strike* (1889). On dockers' living conditions I used *Charles Booth's London*, selected and edited by Albert Freid and R. M. Elman (Hutchinson, 1969); on John Burns, William Kent, *Labour's Lost Leader* (Williams and Norgate, 1950); I also consulted *The Times*; G. D. H. Cole, *Short History*; and Cole and Postgate. The references to the spread of the Dockers' Union after the strike and details of its emblem are quoted by E. J. Hobsbawm (editor) *Labour's Turning Point*, (Lawrence and Wishart, 1948).

CHAPTER FOUR

The best general account, particularly useful on reactions to the outbreak of war, is Robert K. Middlemass, *The Clydesiders*, (Hutchinson, 1965). The most detailed history of the Clydeside Workers Committee is by James Hinton, *The First Shop Stewards' Movement* (Allen and Unwin, 1973), who quotes Lenin's view of Hyndman. The history of the minor left-wing parties in the area, including the influence of Irishmen and Highlanders on political attitudes in Glasgow, is given in great detail by Walter Kendall, *The Revolutionary Movement in Britain 1900–1921* (Weidenfeld and Nicolson, 1969). Nan Milton, *John Maclean* (Pluto Press, 1973) supplied most of the information on her father, while their

respective contributions are described (if not overstated) by David Kirkwood, *My Life of Revolt* (Harrap, 1935), from which I took the account of the Christmas Day meeting and William Gallacher, *Revolt on the Clyde* (Lawrence and Wishart, 1936). On the special situation at Weirs, I consulted W. J. Reader, *Architect of Air Power, The Life of the First Viscount Weir* (Collins, 1968), and the same author's, *The Weir Group, A Centenary History* (Weidenfeld and Nicolson, 1971). On the patriotic response on Clydeside in 1914 and on wartime industry generally I used A. J. P. Taylor, *English History 1914–1945* (O.U.P., 1965). The final anecdote comes from Sir Patrick Hastings, *Autobiography* (Heinemann, 1948).

CHAPTER FIVE

On inter-war economic conditions I used mainly G. P. Jones and A. G. Pool, *A Hundred Years of Economic Development* (Duckworth, 1940) and on general trade union history, Henry Pelling, *A History of British Trade Unionism* (Macmillan, 1972). On events leading up to the General Strike I found Lionel Birch (editor), *The History of the T.U.C. 1868–1968* (T.U.C., 1968) helpful, and on the strike itself, Julian Symons, *The General Strike* (Cresset Press, 1957) and Christopher Farman, *The General Strike* (Panther, 1974), the source of the quotations about contemporary reactions. The railwayman who enjoyed his shorter working day was William John Morgan, *Behind the Steam* (Hutchinson, 1973); on holidays with pay I drew on Charles Loch Mowat, *Britain Between the Wars 1918–1940* (Methuen, 1955) and William Ashworth, *An Economic History of England 1870–1939* (Methuen, 1960). On post-1945 developments and the Labour government's Industrial Relations Bill I consulted Pelling, on the Conservative Industrial Relations Act *Keesings Archives*, and the text of the Act itself. Recent statistics and information about post-war trends in trade unionism were drawn from B. R. Mitchell and H. G. Jones *Second Abstract of British Historical Statistics* (1971); the Department of Employment *Gazette*; the *Report of the Trades Union Congress*, 1974; *British Labour Statistics Yearbook, 1972* (H.M.S.O. 1974) and G. S. Bain, *The Growth of White Collar Unionism* (O.U.P., 1970).